Around-the-World

Moravian Unity Cookbook

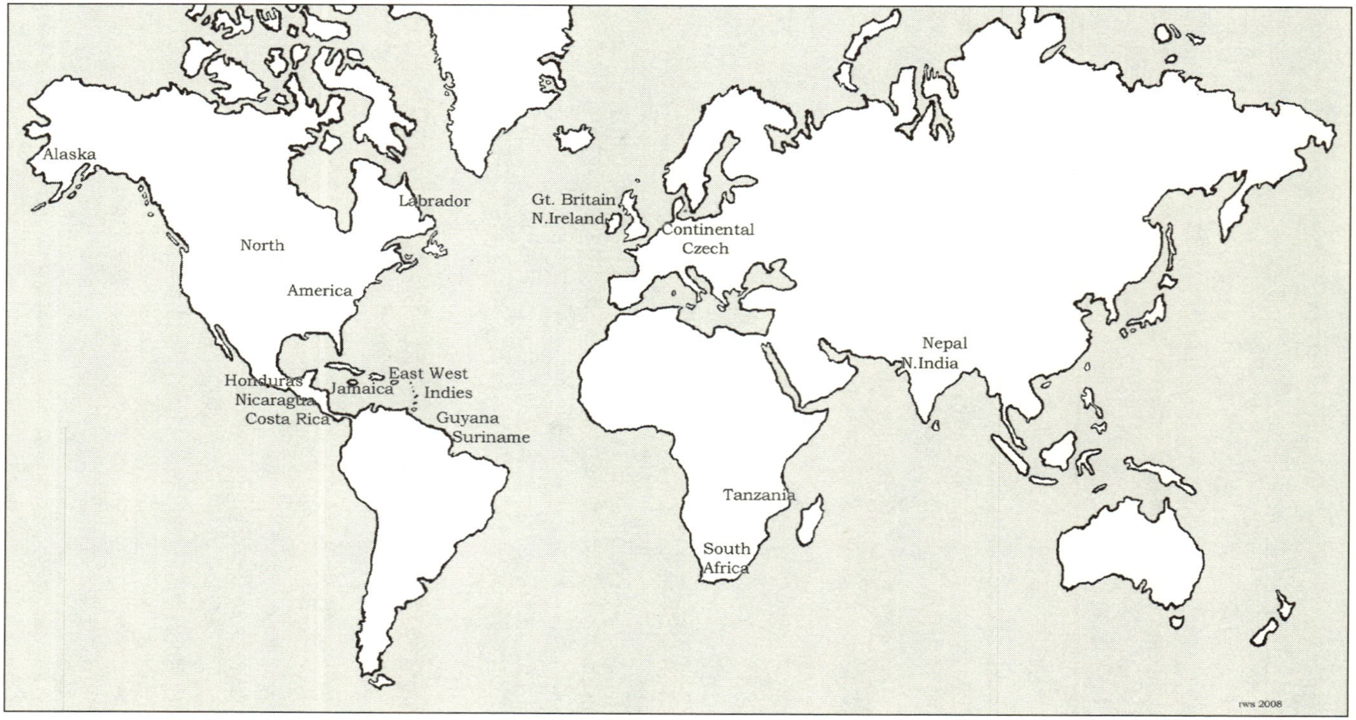
Alaska
Labrador
Gt. Britain
N.Ireland
Continental
Czech
North
America
Nepal
N.India
East West
Indies
Honduras
Nicaragua
Jamaica
Costa Rica
Guyana
Suriname
Tanzania
South
Africa
rws 2008

Around-the-World

Moravian Unity Cookbook

C. Daniel Crews

Moravian Archives
457 S. Church Street
Winston-Salem, North Carolina
www.MoravianArchives.org

© 2008 Moravian Church in America, Southern Province

All rights reserved

Printed in the United States of America

Moravian Archives
457 S. Church Street
Winston-Salem, North Carolina
www.MoravianArchives.org

Library of Congress Control Number: 2008935691

ISBN 978-0-9719411-5-1

The time at dinner or supper is spent neither in silence nor in trifling conversation, but the boys [candidates for ministry] recite from memory either moral precepts or the catechism or hymns or psalms, which they have been directed to learn, but the elder ones repeat some portion of the Scripture, in order.

> — *Ratio Disciplinæ Ordinisque Ecclesiastici in Unitate Fratrum Bohemorum*, 1660
> (*Account of the Ecclesiastical Discipline and Order in the Unity of the Bohemian Brethren*, 1660)
> www.MoravianArchives.org

He giveth food to all flesh: for his mercy endureth for ever.

> — Psalm 136:25

Come, Lord Jesus, our guest to be,
and bless these gifts bestowed by thee.

> — Traditional Moravian table blessing

Contents

Preface ix

Czech Republic 1

Germany and Continental Europe 22

Great Britain and Northern Ireland 45

North America (including Alaska and Labrador) 66

Caribbean Islands and Guyana 88

Suriname 107

Nicaragua, Honduras, Costa Rica 124

South Africa 154

Tanzania and East Africa 184

North India and Nepal 206

Index 229

Preface

The Moravian Church (Unitas Fratrum) is an international church. Numerically, we are small among the denominations of Christendom, but as a Czech Methodist once told me in Prague: "You are small everywhere, but you *are* everywhere!"

It's true. We Moravians live great distances from each other and in a great variety of cultures. And yet one of the great strengths of our church is the friendship, the bond our members share, spanning totally different origins as part of the "Worldwide Unity." Relationships are thus formed which do not deny, but rather go far beyond national and ethnic backgrounds.

We Moravians also like to eat, and to eat appreciatively as we are given to share in God's bounty. The ability to sample and enjoy the food of our Brothers and Sisters in other lands and regions is a sometimes overlooked opportunity to strengthen the ties that bind us together as people of the wondrously diverse world we inhabit. We can all appreciate the old saying: "The family that prays together, stays together." We may go on from this to observe that: "People who eat together, grow together."

The foods we eat and how we like to prepare them are very much a part of who we are. As we share the tables of Moravians in other

AROUND-THE-WORLD MORAVIAN UNITY COOKBOOK

lands or as we enjoy their dishes on our own tables, we find an enjoyable and stimulating means of increasing our mutual understanding. As we recall the 550th anniversary of our church's founding, this seems a particularly good time to bring out a publication such as this.

For the most part, the recipes that follow are not "uniquely Moravian." Moravians have developed a few special dishes in some areas, and we have tried to discover those. Generally, however, these recipes represent a selection of dishes that Moravians may share and enjoy with others in their respective nations, areas, and cultures. This, then, is not a cookbook just for Moravians, but is for all who want to appreciate the cuisine and wider insights of people of other lands.

As here presented, these recipes, unless otherwise noted, are my own practical adaptation or collation of traditional ones. In several cases, I have substituted ingredients and cooking methods more readily available in North America. Along with preparation hints, I have also in many cases suggested variations that may turn a given recipe into two or three or more different dishes. The recipes generally serve four people with hearty appetites, and can be expanded or halved as necessary. As you try them yourself, feel free to adapt or substitute similar ingredients. In so doing, you will add your own bit to the richness of our common heritage. After all, not everyone in the Southern Province in the U.S.A. makes chicken pie in exactly the same way (opinions as to the *right* way, i.e., "like Grandma did it," notwithstanding).

Thanks are due to many persons in various parts of the world who shared their favorite recipes with us. Many of these are noted in the text. The Board of World Mission helped us gather many of these, and deserves thanks also. A portion of any profits from this publica-

Preface

tion will be shared with the Mission Board for agricultural, relief, service, or other ministries as needed.

I especially appreciate the willingness of the Southern Archives, Music Foundation, and Mission Board staffs to be "guinea pigs" for many of these recipes. On the other hand, they didn't seem to regard this as a hardship.

Special thanks are also due to my wife, Sarah, who not only tasted her way through various trial versions of these dishes, but also helped me surf the Internet to get ideas for recipes I didn't have access to otherwise. Copyrights have not been infringed, of course, but some of these helped point me in the right direction in several areas.

Finally, there are obviously many more recipes that deserve inclusion in a work such as this. We have only scratched our culinary surface. Our hope is to give a far wider selection in a later expanded edition or perhaps a second volume. If you have recipes you would like to see included, please send them to us at dcrews@mcsp.org. In the meantime, cook, enjoy, and share in the gifts our Lord has given us in our worldwide Unity.

C. Daniel Crews, Archivist
Moravian Church in America, Southern Province
Winston-Salem, North Carolina
September 2008

Around-the-World

Moravian Unity Cookbook

The Czech Republic

(Bohemia and Moravia)

Our church had its beginnings in these lands 550 years ago. It was destroyed and banned in its homelands in the Thirty Years War of 1618-48. Not until the 1870s were we allowed to establish congregations there again.

I was fortunate to learn many of these dishes from Sr. Marie Ulrichová, wife of Bishop Adolf Ulrich, while I was studying at the University of Prague in 1977. These foods are of particular meaning to all of us, since they are the sort of thing Hus and Comenius would have enjoyed.

Cheese Spread
(Liptovský Sýr)

This makes a great appetizer or snack. Spread it on small pieces of rye or pumpernickel bread.

1 (8 oz.) pkg. cream cheese
1 T. onion, finely grated
¼ tsp. Dijon or brown mustard
1 tsp. capers
1 T. pickle relish
½ tsp. paprika

Soften the cream cheese so you can mix and spread it. (A minute on defrost in the microwave works well.) Chop the capers and relish fine.

Mix all ingredients together. This is better if it has a couple of hours of rest for the flavors to blend.

Cucumber Salad
(Okurková Salát)

½ European or "English" cucumber
1 T. powdered sugar
1 T. malt vinegar
1 T. white vinegar
½ tsp. salt
1 cup cold water

Peel the cucumber and slice very thin, ⅛ inch or less. In a bowl put powdered sugar, the vinegars, and salt. Stir until sugar is mostly dissolved. Add water, stir, and then add the cucumber slices. Let stand for a half hour or more. Serve each portion in its own little bowl to accompany meats, etc.

Plain Salad
(Hlávkový Salát)

The Czech name literally means "head salad." Don't worry, it's heads of lettuce that this refers to. Just get some fresh heads of Boston lettuce, break them up, and pour on some of the same "plain" salad dressing used with the cucumbers above.

Goulash Soup
(Gulášová Polévka)

2 onions, chopped
4 T. butter
2 tsp. paprika
1 pound beef stew meat,
    cut in small pieces
3 T. flour

4 cups beef broth
1½ cups diced vegetables
    (carrot, celery, parsnip, etc.)
2 medium potatoes, diced
¼ tsp. caraway seeds (optional)
salt and pepper to taste

Fry onion in the butter. Add paprika and beef. Cook until meat begins to brown. Add flour and brown, stirring constantly. Add carrots, celery, etc., salt and pepper, and cook for 10 to 12 minutes. Pour in broth. Add potatoes and caraway seeds and simmer until potatoes are tender (another 20 minutes). The caraway seeds lend character to the soup, but leave them out if you don't like them.

White Soup
(Bilá Polévka)

This soup is a lot more interesting than its name sounds. It is made by combining whatever vegetables are left over from the day before with a rich cream base. It is a staple in workers' cafes.

2 T. butter	1 (15½ oz.) can chicken broth
½ onion, chopped	1 cup whole milk or cream
1 T. flour	¼ tsp. thyme
1 cup leftover cooked vegetables (carrots, celery, potatoes, limas, cauliflower, etc.)	¼ tsp. seasoned salt
	salt and pepper to taste
	parsley, chopped (optional)

Melt butter in pot and cook onion on medium low heat until soft but not browned. Add flour and cook for a minute until flour has absorbed butter but is not browned. Add vegetables. (Canned or frozen "mixed vegetables" will do if you don't have leftovers. If using frozen, cook the vegetables before adding to soup.) Add broth and heat just to boiling. Reduce heat and add milk or cream. Add seasonings, stir, and serve. Garnish with chopped parsley if you like.

Braised Beef and Sour Cream
(Svíčková na Smetaně)

The Czech name for this dish means "Little Candles with Cream." The slices of beef are about the size and shape of small candles. Traditionally this is made with beef tenderloin, but London broil is affordable and works well. It is usually served with dumplings (knedliky, page 12) and sautéed sauerkraut (page 14). Cucumber salad (page 3) can replace the kraut. It is rich and comforting either way.

1½ to 2 pounds beef
    (London broil or similar)
¼ cup malt vinegar
1 cup water
3 T. butter, oil, or mixture
2½ cups diced onion, carrot,
    celery, parsnip, etc., mixture
2 cups beef broth

¼ to ½ tsp. coarse black pepper
¼ tsp. ground allspice
1 bay leaf
¼ tsp. dried thyme
2 T. flour
salt to taste
3 T. sour cream

Place beef, vinegar, and water into a zip-top plastic bag and let marinate in refrigerator for 1 to 3 hours. Remove beef and pat dry. Discard marinade. In an ovenproof heavy pan or casserole brown the beef on all sides with the vegetables in the butter or oil. Add seasonings, salt, and ½ cup of broth. Cover and roast in preheated 350° oven until tender (about 45 minutes). Check after half an hour to make sure the pan isn't drying out. If it is, add a little water. When meat is done, remove it to a platter. Take out bay leaf, mix flour with a little water and add to pan. Stir. Add rest of broth and stir to make gravy. Place gravy in blender and puree (smooth or a little chunky as you like). You will need to do this in two lots. Return gravy to pan over low heat and stir in sour cream. Stir until smooth. Slice beef into ¼- to ½-inch slices and pour some gravy on top. Serve remainder of gravy on the side (for dumplings, noodles, etc.).

Roast Pork
(Vepřová Pečeně)

This and Svíčková may not be the official national dishes, but they do represent the plain, hearty, and flavorful cooking which characterizes the Czechs. Noodles or boiled potatoes or of course knedliky (page 12) go well with it. Add a soup or salad with plain dressing (page 3) and braised sauerkraut (page 14), and you have a meal well worth the eating.

> 2 pounds pork loin
> salt and pepper to taste
> ½ tsp. caraway seeds
> 1½ to 2 cups broth (beef, chicken, or mixed)

Preheat oven to 350°.

Score fat on meat crosswise. Sprinkle meat all over with salt, pepper, and caraway seeds. Place on rack in roasting pan and add half the broth. Roast in preheated 350° oven for 1 hour or until nice and done. Baste every 15 minutes or so, and add broth as needed to keep the bottom of the pan from burning. The resulting drippings make a nice gravy if you stir them with a little more broth or water into 1 T. flour which has been lightly browned in 1 T. butter.

Veal Paprika
(Telecí Maso na Paprice)

This is similar to Hungarian goulash, but has its own character. Lamb, beef, or pork can be used in place of the veal, but you will need to braise these meats longer and add more liquid to get them really tender. This goes especially well with egg noodles.

1½ pounds veal stew meat, cubed	2 tsp. paprika
4 T. butter	1 T. flour
1 tsp. garlic, minced (optional)	2 cups chicken broth (divided)
1 medium onion, diced	salt and pepper to taste
	½ cup sour cream

Fry meat in butter until it begins to brown. Add onion (and garlic) and brown slightly. Sprinkle with salt and pepper. Pour in ½ cup of broth. Cover and braise on medium low heat for 20 minutes or until meat is tender. Check halfway through, and then every few minutes. If it starts to burn, add a little water. When meat is tender, increase heat and allow any liquid to evaporate.

Add paprika and flour. Cook until flour is browned. Add the rest of the broth and stir until gravy thickens. Reduce heat and add sour cream.

Chicken Paprika
(Kuře na Paprice)

This is similar to veal paprika above. Indeed, you can use the above recipe and substitute cubed boneless, skinless chicken breast for the veal. More traditionally, though, a whole chicken is cut into pieces and browned with the onion in butter. The heat is reduced, and all the broth is added. The dish then simmers for a half hour to 45 minutes until the chicken is tender. Then the chicken is removed from the pan and placed on a serving platter. The sour cream is mixed into the flour, and this is stirred into the liquid. The heat is increased, and the gravy cooks until thickened. It is then poured over the chicken pieces.

Spanish Birds
(Španělští Ptací)

Contrary to the name, these rolls are neither Spanish nor birds. Perhaps the shape of these trussed up meat rolls suggested a small braised quail or something similar. We will not even speculate on why the Czechs thought it would be a good idea to boil Spaniards in tomato sauce.

8 small thinly sliced (⅛ to ¼ inch) beef bottom round or "sandwich" steaks
salt and pepper to taste
8 dill pickle spears
3 T. butter
1 onion, diced
½ bell pepper, diced
2 cups tomato sauce
2 tsp. Worcestershire sauce
garlic powder, onion powder, paprika to taste

Season both sides of meat with salt and pepper to taste. Take a pickle spear and roll it inside the meat to make a cylinder. Tie with twine or use toothpicks to secure.

Melt butter in heavy pan, and sear meat rolls on all sides until they are nicely browned. Remove from pan.

Add more butter to pan if necessary to make 2 T. Fry onion and pepper until the pieces begin to brown. Add tomato sauce and Worcestershire sauce. Season to taste with garlic and onion powder, etc. Be generous with paprika.

Reduce to simmer and put meat back in pan. Braise for 20 minutes or so until meat is done through. Turn occasionally as they cook.

Remove twine or toothpicks. Serve with mashed potatoes, cucumber salad, etc.

Fried Cheese
(Smažený Sýr)

Meat has not always been plentiful on Czech tables. This makes a good substitute for hard times or when a lighter meal is desired. It tastes great at any time. Boiled potatoes usually accompany the cheese as does a tasty tartar sauce (included here).

8 to 12 slices Gouda or Muenster cheese, cut about ½ inch thick
salt and pepper
½ cup flour
1 egg, beaten with a little water
½ cup breadcrumbs
oil for frying

Roll cheese on all sides in salted and peppered flour. Dip in egg, then roll in breadcrumbs to cover all sides. Fry quickly in hot oil to brown before the cheese melts too much (only about a minute a side). It is wise to do the frying in two or three batches to avoid a disastrous meltdown. Serve while center of cheese is warm and gooey.

Hints: If you have trouble with the cheese melting before the breadcrumbs brown, put it into the freezer for a few minutes before dipping in egg, etc. Also if you have to cook this dish ahead of time, pop it in the microwave on medium power for 10 seconds right before serving, and it will become gooey again.

Tartar Sauce: Mix together ½ cup mayonnaise, 1 T. sour cream, ¾ tsp. chopped parsley, 2 tsp. finely minced pickle, 1 T. finely minced onion, and 1 tsp. chopped capers. I like to add a dash of garlic powder as well, but it's your choice.

Boiled Potatoes
(Brambory)

This is simplicity itself. Just peel a medium potato for each person, cut into ½- to ¾-inch cubes and boil in well-salted water for 15 minutes or so until potatoes are tender. What makes them special is to add a T. or so of caraway seeds to the water as they cook.

Cheese-Stuffed Potatoes
(Brambory Plněné Sýrem)

4 baked potatoes, still warm
4 T. butter
4 T. sour cream
⅔ cup grated cheese (divided)
2 egg yolks
1 tsp. garlic powder
1 T. paprika
salt and pepper to taste
2 tsp. chives, chopped

Preheat oven to 350°.

When potatoes are cool enough to handle, cut a wide strip of skin off the top of each. Scoop out the insides (and place in a bowl), being careful not to tear through the skin and leaving about ¼-inch wall all around. Set shells aside.

Mash the potato in the bowl, and stir in butter, sour cream, and ½ cup of the cheese. Stir in egg yolks (these go in last so they won't curdle from the heat). Stir in garlic powder, paprika (save a little for garnish later), and salt and pepper.

Stuff shells with this mixture. Place them open side up in an ovenware dish, and bake in preheated 350° oven for 20 minutes. Sprinkle the rest of the cheese, paprika, and the chives on top, and return to oven for another 10 minutes or so until top is slightly browned.

Dumplings
(Knedliky)

These are the quintessential Czech accompaniment to meat and gravy. In fact, knedliky *require* gravy. In the Czech lands they are made with yeast, rolled into small logs, allowed to rise, boiled in water and then sliced with a wire or strong thread. American flour, however, is different from Czech, so that method doesn't work as well here. Still, where there is a will, there is usually a way, albeit a bit unorthodox.

1 (¼ oz.) pkg. dry yeast
2 T. warm water
1 tsp. sugar
1 cup regular flour
1 cup cake flour

½ cup milk
½ tsp. salt
1 egg yolk
½ cup cubed stale bread
1 tsp. butter

Dissolve the yeast in a little warm water with the sugar. Allow to "proof" as you get the other ingredients ready.

Place the flours in a large bowl. Warm the milk 20 seconds or so in microwave to knock the chill off, then stir in salt and egg yolk. Pour milk mixture over flour. Add yeast mixture. Stir to make a soft dough. Knead until the dough holds together well (10 minutes or as long as you can hold out; a stand mixer with a dough hook is a godsend).

Cover and let stand in a warm place for an hour or so until the dough has doubled in size. Fry the bread cubes in the butter until they brown a little. Let cool. When dough is risen, push down and mix in the bread cubes so they are fairly well distributed throughout the dough.

Dust your hands in flour, or wet them with water, and separate the dough into 2 equal pieces. Roll each piece into a log about 8 or 9 inches long. You can cook these rolls whole in simmering water for a half hour or until they float and are firm. Remove from water and cut into ½-inch rounds.

Or: Here is the really unorthodox suggestion. Wrap each uncooked log (loosely!) in wax paper. (A light coat of cooking spray on the inside of the wax paper will make sure the dough doesn't stick.) Let stand for several minutes to begin to rise again. Then put them in a microwave and cook them on high for 4 minutes. Carefully remove the wax paper to let the steam out, and let the logs cool until you can handle them. Then slice into ½-inch rounds. Voila! Knedliky!!!

Sautéed Sauerkraut
(Dušené Kyselé Zelí)

This is a great accompaniment to meat. Cooking the kraut removes the harshness and makes it mellow. Many who "don't like kraut" find this a pleasant surprise.

1 small onion, diced	1 T. flour
2 T. butter	1 T. brown sugar
1 (15½ oz.) can sauerkraut	½ cup water
1 tsp. caraway seeds	

Fry onion in butter to soften but not brown. Add kraut, caraway, flour, and sugar. Stir to mix and cook on low heat for 5 minutes. Add water and stir until sauce thickens.

Braised Cabbage
(Zelí Dušené)

This is a good side dish, particularly for those who still can't take the kraut given above. This is Marie Ulrichová's personal recipe.

2 T. vegetable oil
1 medium onion
1 medium or ½ large head
    white or green cabbage
½ tsp. caraway seeds

½ tsp. salt
2 tsp. flour
1 T. malt vinegar
1 tsp. sugar

In a large Dutch oven heat oil over medium high heat. Add onion, finely sliced. Cook until onion is softened but not brown. Cut cabbage into thin strips and add to oil and onion with caraway seeds and salt. Pour in ½ cup water, reduce heat to medium, and stew for 20 minutes. Stir occasionally and add a little more water if pot is going dry. Add flour, stir, and cook 5 more minutes. Add vinegar and sugar. Stir, check for seasoning, and serve.

Compare this with the Tanzanian braised cabbage (page 200).

Creamed Vegetables
(Zeleny na Smetaně)

The following sauce goes well with a variety of cooked vegetables: spinach, Brussels sprouts, green beans, peas, asparagus, etc. This recipe makes enough sauce for four 2½-3 oz. servings of vegetables.

2 T. butter
½ tsp. sugar
dash of nutmeg (freshly
 grated if possible)

salt and pepper to taste
2 tsp. flour
½ cup heavy cream

Melt butter in a saucepan over medium heat. Add sugar, nutmeg, and salt and pepper. Place flour in a cup and add part of the cream to dissolve. Pour into pan and add remaining cream. Stir to heat through and thicken. If it gets too thick, add a little milk. Vegetables can be simmered in the sauce for a few minutes, or served plain and the sauce poured over them.

Apricot Mousse

Many Czechs are particularly fond of apricots. This is a refreshing light dessert. Original recipes call for fresh apricots peeled, seeded, and boiled in sugar water, then mixed with unflavored gelatin, etc. The following is easier but comes out just as good.

>1 cup apricot nectar
>1 (3 oz.) pkg. apricot gelatin dessert
>1 cup whipping cream

Bring apricot nectar to a boil, then mix thoroughly into gelatin dessert powder. (**Do not** add the water called for on the box.) Beat with a mixer to make sure all the powder is dissolved. Let cool to near room temperature.

Whip cream into stiff peaks. Gently fold gelatin mixture into cream. Again, be sure it is evenly mixed. This will take a little while.

Pour into a bowl and refrigerate for about 3 hours until set. You can also put it into a mold. To unmold, dip mold into hot water for 15 seconds, put a plate over the top, and invert.

Decorate if you wish with canned apricot halves and more whipped cream.

Sacher Torte
(Sachrův Dort)

This famous cake, of course, originated at the Sacher Hotel in Vienna. Despite its Austrian origins, it became a favorite for special occasions in the Czech lands.

Cake:

3 oz. semisweet chocolate, melted
5 T. butter, softened
½ cup sugar

6 eggs, separated
⅔ cup flour
¼ cup slivered almonds
3 T. apricot jam

Icing:

½ cup sugar
3 T. water
4 oz. semisweet chocolate, melted

2 tsp. butter, softened
vanilla (optional)

Making the cake:

Preheat oven to 350°.

Melt chocolate over boiling water or in microwave.

While chocolate is melting, beat butter and sugar together until light and creamy. Beat in the egg yolks one or two at a time. Add warm (but not too hot) chocolate and stir until completely blended.

Beat the egg whites to form stiff peaks. Chop the almonds into small pieces and mix into flour. (Be sure the almond pieces get well coated with the flour or they will sink in the batter.)

Fold the egg whites into the sugar, egg, and chocolate mixture. Then carefully fold in the flour and almonds. Some recipes call for alternating the egg whites and flour during the folding process.

Put batter into a 9-inch greased and floured pan (a springform one works best), and bake in a preheated 350° oven for about 40 minutes. When toothpick or thin knife inserted into the center comes out clean, the cake is done. Let cool a bit, remove from pan, and then spread apricot jam over top of cake. Let cool more before icing it.

For icing: The most traditional way is to cook the water and sugar together until they reach 230° to 234° ("thread stage"). Let this solution cool until it is warm, but no longer hot. Mix chocolate and butter, and then slowly pour sugar solution into chocolate, stirring constantly. Add a dash of vanilla if you like. Pour and spread on cake immediately. This icing sets up very quickly, so you have to work fast. If it sets up before you are done, try adding 1 T. vegetable oil and reheating it slowly in the microwave.

A safer icing option is to melt 8 oz. of *bittersweet* chocolate into ¾ cup of heavy or whipping cream (or ¼ lb. melted butter and ½ cup water). Let cool a little, and pour that evenly over the cake.

Czech Buns
(Kolačky)

2 T. warm water
1 T. sugar
1 (¼ oz.) pkg. dry yeast
1 cup cake flour
1¼ cups regular flour
3 T. sugar

½ tsp. salt
½ cup warm milk
2 T. butter, melted
1 egg
½ tsp. vanilla

Basic Dough:

Mix water, the 1 T. sugar, and yeast. Let sit to "proof" while you assemble the rest of the ingredients.

Combine yeast mixture and dry and wet ingredients in a stand mixer if you have one. Otherwise stir with a spoon until all is thoroughly mixed. Knead for several minutes. The dough will be very soft. If it is too soupy, add a T. or two more flour.

Cover and put in a warm place to rise until doubled in size, at least an hour.

Flour a flat surface well, turn out dough, and with well-floured hands pat out to about ½ inch thickness.

Filling suggestions:

For "Bohemia style" buns, cut into 2½- to 3-inch squares. Put a rounded teaspoon of jam or preserves in the center of each. (Apricot is a favorite, but strawberry, cherry, and peach are good too. If you can find poppy seed filling, that is a favorite also.) Dough will still be very soft, so flour your hands again, and turn up corners, pinching edges to seal jam, etc., inside.

For "Moravia style" buns, cut into 2½- to 3-inch circles. Mix 4 T. ricotta cheese, 2 T. sugar, and ¼ tsp. vanilla, and put a rounded tsp. of mixture in the center of each. Seal as above. Then make an indentation in the top center of each, and put in a tsp. of your favorite jam, etc.

Baking:

Place buns on baking sheet, cover loosely, and let rise in a warm place for 45 minutes or so. Brush tops with milk or melted butter.

Bake in a preheated 325° oven until lightly browned, 20 minutes or so. Check halfway through to make sure they are baking evenly. Rotate pan if necessary.

Allow to cool for 15 to 20 minutes and sprinkle tops with powdered sugar.

Germany and the European Continental Province

It was in Germany that the Moravian Church got a fresh start in the 1720s. Exiles from Moravia and others found refuge on the estate of Count Nicholas Ludwig von Zinzendorf and founded the village of Herrnhut in 1722. There the Unity was renewed, and several more settlements were established in Germany, the Netherlands, Denmark, and Switzerland. Missionaries and settlers went out to the Caribbean, North America, and South Africa, giving the Moravian Church the international character it has today. Here are a few dishes from our church's "second homeland."

Pickled Herring
(Rollmops or Matjes)

Pickled herring in several forms is a popular appetizer or snack. Original recipes call for cleaning fresh fish or soaking salt herring for days. Fortunately, already pickled herring is generally available now in grocery stores or specialty shops.

The plain pickled fish can be given a special twist by taking larger fillets, spreading them with brown mustard, some thinly sliced sour pickles, thinly sliced onion, and a few capers. Then roll them up, secure with a toothpick, and return them to the juice they came in.

Roy Ledbetter, who served in Königsfeld in the late 1970s, brought back a Moravian treatment from Sr. Erdmuth Dorothea Munk. Chop pickled herring into bite-size pieces and set aside. Combine equal amounts of sour cream and mayonnaise, stir in a little salt and pepper, sweet paprika, dill (weed), and just a pinch of sugar. Add rings of sliced onion and wedges of sliced apple. Gently stir in herring pieces. Cover, refrigerate, and let stand for a few hours (or overnight) to blend flavors. Serve with rye or pumpernickel bread.

For an appetizer tray, the herring can be served with slices of sausage, cubes of Swiss or Muenster cheese, etc., along with the bread.

Mixed Salad

In Germany and elsewhere in Europe (except in restaurants catering to American tourists) salad does not mean a big bowl of lettuce with slices of tomato, cucumber, onions, and croutons. Instead, various vegetables are sliced thin or cut into small sticks, and a little light dressing (see below) is poured over them. Raw carrots, cucumbers, radishes, red cabbage, and small tomatoes are favorites. Steamed vegetables, such as asparagus and beets, are used as well. A "mixed salad" consists of little piles of individual vegetables spread around the edge of a small plate with a little dressing in the middle or poured over each vegetable. Choice of vegetables is whatever you have or like.

Salad Dressing: Whisk together three parts light salad oil to two parts vinegar or lemon juice and a pinch of salt. Dried herbs can be added to taste. Sour cream (equal in amount to the vinegar) and a little sugar can be added for variation.

Pickled Red Cabbage

This can be served cold as part of a "mixed salad" or warm as a side dish with meat.

½ head red cabbage	2 T. salad oil
2 strips bacon	2 T. vinegar
1 cup water	salt and pepper
¼ tsp. salt	1 apple
1 T. sugar	

Remove the core and finely slice or chop the cabbage. Cut bacon into small pieces and fry until crisp. Add cabbage, stir, and let cook for a couple of minutes. Add water and salt. Let come to a boil, then reduce heat to medium, cover, and let simmer for about 15 minutes or until cabbage is tender. Increase heat to evaporate any excess moisture (there should be a little liquid left), then add sugar, oil, and vinegar, and season to taste. Core and dice apple, add to cabbage, and stir until apple begins to take on red color. Let stand a half hour or more for flavors to blend. Serve warm or cold.

Potato Soup

There are countless variations to this recipe. Every area and practically every family does it differently. This is a good one, but feel free to add or subtract to make it your own.

3 good-size potatoes
2 cups beef or chicken broth
1 medium onion
½ cup mixed carrots, celery, etc., diced small
3 strips bacon
1 cup milk or light cream
salt and pepper to taste
scant ¼ tsp. nutmeg
chives to garnish

Peel potatoes and cut into small cubes. Put in pot with the broth and bring to boil, then reduce heat to medium low. Finely dice onion and other vegetables and add to potatoes as they cook. Fry bacon crisp, remove strips from grease, and add grease to potatoes. (You can substitute 1 T. butter for the bacon grease if you prefer.) After 15 minutes check to see if potatoes are tender. If not, cook a few minutes more. With a potato masher, mash potatoes and vegetables, but leave enough pieces to give the soup some texture. Add milk or cream and heat almost to boiling. Add salt and pepper to taste, along with nutmeg. Serve in bowls and garnish with crumbled bacon and chives.

Variations: Other soups can be made by using leeks or lentils instead of the potatoes. Use three leeks (white part only, thinly sliced and rinsed to remove any sand). Omit the mashing. The leek version will also need 2 tsp. cornstarch dissolved in a little cold water to thicken it before the milk is added. Fresh lentils (1 cup) should be cooked in water for about a half hour first. A 15 oz. can of lentils, drained, works fine also.

Dutch Pea Soup

Paul Peucker, Moravian Archivist in Bethlehem, Pennsylvania, who was born in the Netherlands, sends this typical Dutch recipe. Paul says it "is traditionally eaten in the winter after ice skating."

1 oz. split peas	1 large carrot (about ½ oz.)
1 oz. pork shoulder chop	½ celeriac (celery root)
1 T. salt	2 thin leeks
pepper	2 to 3 oz. smoked sausage
1 bay leaf	5 twigs of celery
2 onions	

Wash the peas. Combine the peas, the shoulder chop, and 9 cups of water (2 liters). Add salt, pepper, and bay leaf. Bring to boil on medium heat and let simmer for about 15 minutes.

Peel and dice the onions. Wash and dice the carrot and celeriac. Wash and cut the leeks in rings.

Add the onion, carrot, celeriac, and leeks to the soup. Bring it to boil again, and let it softly boil for another half hour. Stir. Add the sausage for about 10 minutes.

Take out the shoulder chop and sausage from the soup. Remove the bay leaf. Cut the meat into small pieces and return to the soup. Cut up the celery over the soup and add salt and pepper. It is now ready to serve.

Blue Trout
(Forelle Blau)

This is a favorite and colorful way to prepare trout. The vinegar is what turns the skin blue. In some restaurants they have a tank of live fish so you can select your own for dinner. Traditionally, the heads are left on, but if food staring at you from your plate is a problem, they can be removed.

1 cup vinegar	1 bay leaf
3 cups water	4 whole trout, cleaned
1 onion, thinly sliced	salt and pepper to taste

Bring vinegar and water to simmer. Add onion and bay leaf. Add fish and allow to poach for about 10 minutes. Remove fish from poaching liquid, drain, and season with salt and pepper. A vegetable salad and boiled potatoes with butter go well with this. A squeeze of lemon over the fish is optional. You may find the vinegar gives it enough of a tang.

Farmer's Treat
(Bauernschmaus)

This was developed from peasant food, but you may find it as a specialty in a chain of family restaurants in Germany. It's easy to make at home, and it will pleasantly fill you up in no time.

4 strips bacon (plus 2 T. vegetable oil for frying)	1 medium onion, chopped
	1 tsp. garlic, chopped
3 boneless, skinless chicken breasts	1 cup or more chicken broth
	salt and pepper to taste
3 good-size potatoes	parsley for garnish

In a large pan fry bacon until crisp. Remove bacon strips, leaving the fat. Bacon is leaner these days, so if the bacon does not render much fat, add oil to the pan to make 2 T.

Cut chicken into bite-size pieces and fry in bacon fat (and oil) until they begin to brown. Remove chicken and set aside. If pan is dry, add another T. oil. Cut potatoes into large cubes and add to pan with chopped onion and garlic. Fry in bacon fat and oil until they take on a golden brown color.

Put chicken back in pan with potatoes and onion. Pour in 1 cup broth and simmer (stirring occasionally) until potatoes are tender (15 to 20 minutes). Potatoes will absorb some of the broth. If they start to get dry, add more broth. At the end of the cooking the chicken, potatoes, and onions should be moist but not swimming in liquid. Crumble bacon and add to mixture. Check for seasoning and serve with parsley for garnish.

This dish is traditionally further seasoned with *Maggi*® seasoning sauce. This is a commercial brand. If you can't find it, try combining ¼ cup water, 1 tsp. soy sauce, and 2 drops each of Worcestershire sauce, malt vinegar, and liquid smoke. It won't be quite the same, but it's close and is still good. Use a few drops or more, as you like.

Sauerbraten

This is one of those dishes that everyone has heard of but few have actually sampled. Now you can. Just remember to plan ahead since the meat needs to marinate for a few days.

2 lb. piece London broil or chuck roast
1 onion, sliced
6 peppercorns
3 cloves
2 bay leaves
¾ cup vinegar

1½ cups water
2 T. oil or butter
1 to 2 cups beef broth
2 gingersnaps
1½ tsp. cornstarch
salt and pepper to taste

Place meat in zip-top plastic bag with onion, peppercorns, cloves, bay leaves, vinegar, and water. Let marinate in refrigerator for three to four days. Turn it over a couple of times every day.

Remove meat, pat dry, and brown in oil or butter on all sides in large pan. Add 1 cup beef broth and bring to simmer. Put in gingersnaps. Let braise for about 45 minutes to an hour. Add more broth if it starts to go dry. Remove meat and put on platter. Dissolve cornstarch in a little cold water, and stir into pan to thicken gravy. Check for seasoning.

When meat has rested for 10 minutes or more, cut it into ¼- to ½-inch slices. The gravy can be passed in a bowl for all to add as much as they like. Store-bought egg noodles go well with this, but potato dumplings (page 35) bring it to perfection.

Meatballs with Capers
(Königsberger Klopse)

This dish is named after the city of Königsberg, which passed to Russian control after World War II. The dish remains, however, and makes an occasional change from our favorite spaghetti and meatballs.

1 lb. ground beef (or mixed beef, pork, or veal)	salt and pepper to taste
	2 cups beef broth
4 slices stale bread torn up and soaked in ¼ cup milk, then squeezed dry	2 T. butter
	2 T. flour
	1 T. capers
¼ cup onion, grated	2 tsp. lemon juice
1 egg	

Mix meat, bread, onion, egg, and salt and pepper. Knead well and make into 12 balls. Bring broth to a boil and drop in meatballs. Reduce heat and simmer for 15 minutes. In a separate pan make a roux by cooking butter and flour for a minute or so, then add to broth, stirring to blend until gravy thickens. Add capers and lemon juice.

These are good over egg noodles or with potato dumplings (page 35).

Brootjes

These are a very popular snack or street food in the Netherlands. Get small (3-inch or so) sandwich rolls. Slice and spread with butter. Fill with Gouda cheese or ham or a combination. Add a slice of tomato if you like.

Sausages

Grilled sausages are good anywhere. You can make your own if you have the time and equipment, but good commercial bratwurst, knockwurst, etc., are readily available. (Note: "Wurst" is pronounced "voorst," *not* "worst.") Instead of simply pricking a few holes in the casing to let out steam and grease, sausages are often cut with a cross right on the ends, so that after grilling the ends make a little "flower." Serve them with brown mustard and fried potatoes (page 33).

Fried Potatoes
(Pommes Frites)

These are similar to American French fries, but have their own character. Peel a potato for each portion and cut them into ⅜-inch wide strips (like French fries). Cut strips into 1¼-inch lengths. Cover bottom of large heavy skillet with oil and heat to frying temperature (about 350°). Add potatoes but don't overcrowd pan. It's better to do this in separate lots for more than two portions. Allow the potatoes to cook for 4 to 5 minutes, until the bottoms begin to color. Then start to turn them so all sides can brown. (This takes some patience.) When the potatoes are a golden brown, taste one to make sure they are cooked through. (Run some water over it to cool it enough so you don't burn your mouth.) If it is still crunchy inside, reduce heat, keep stirring, and cook a few minutes more. When they are done, remove from pan with a slotted spoon, place on paper towels to drain, and sprinkle with salt immediately.

Potato Pancakes
(Kartoffelpuffer)

These make another good accompaniment to sausages, or as a light meal on their own served with applesauce, a dollop of sour cream, and a salad.

2 eggs	¼ cup flour
1 small onion, peeled	salt and pepper to taste
4 medium potatoes	oil for frying

Break the eggs into a small bowl and beat. Grate the onion and squeeze out excess moisture in a paper towel. Peel and grate the potatoes. Put a damp paper towel over the already grated potatoes as you go so they won't turn brown. Squeeze potatoes to remove moisture. Mix all ingredients (except oil) and form into 8 to 12 pancakes. Fry in hot oil, turning to get nice and crispy brown on both sides. Add more oil if needed. When done, remove pancakes from oil with a spatula or slotted spoon, drain, and sprinkle with a little more salt.

Potato Salad

This is a warm sweet-and-sour dish. It goes well with sausages, meats, and chicken.

4 slices bacon	3 T. vinegar
4 medium potatoes	2 T. sugar
salt and pepper to taste	chopped parsley for garnish
1 medium onion	

Fry bacon until crisp, remove from pan, and save grease. Peel potatoes, cut into ¼- to ⅓-inch slices, and boil in salted water until tender but still holding together (about 12 minutes). Remove from pot and drain. Add bacon grease to pot (and enough extra oil to make 2 T.). Peel and slice onion thin, and fry in oil until soft but not brown. Add vinegar, sugar, and crumbled bacon. Mix in potatoes. Add pepper and a little salt if needed. Garnish with parsley.

Potato Dumplings
(Klösse)

These are wonderful with meat and lots of gravy. They are also very filling, so a couple of them go a long way.

4 medium potatoes (about 2 lbs.)	7 T. potato starch, divided
2 eggs	¾ cup flour
pinch of nutmeg	8 croutons (or toasted
salt to taste	cubes of bread)

Boil potatoes in their jackets 30 minutes or until a fork goes in easily. Let cool enough to handle, then peel. Refrigerate overnight. (This allows the starch in the potatoes to set properly.) Then run potatoes through a food mill, or grate and mash. Add the eggs, nutmeg, and salt. Mix well. Add 5 T. potato starch and flour, mix well, and let rest 1 hour. Flour hands with potato starch and divide dough into 8 equal portions. Press a crouton into the center of each piece and roll to make a ball. Roll balls in potato starch. Boil in large pot uncovered for about 5 minutes (until balls float). Reduce heat, partially cover, and cook for 10 minutes. Remove with slotted spoon. Allow to drain, and serve with meat and gravy. You can garnish the dish with parsley if you like.

Spätzle

These are little dumplings that can be served in soups or as a starch in place of potatoes or bigger dumplings. (**Note:** The name is pronounced "schpet-zleh," not "spet-zel" as is often butchered by TV cooks.) It means "little sparrows," but no one seems to know why they are called this. They are made in various ways, but this is a version supplied by Roy Ledbetter.

½ cup milk or buttermilk
2 large eggs
⅔ tsp. salt

dash of nutmeg
1⅓ cups flour

Bring a large pot of salted water to the boil. It should be boiling already when the batter is ready for it.

Combine milk, eggs, salt, and nutmeg; blend until smooth. Add flour and beat together until batter is smooth. Batter will be thick and sticky, but still liquid.

Drop the batter into the boiling water a little at a time. You can do this by pushing batter through the large holes in a box grater or ricer. Some folks put the batter on a plate, push a little over the side, and cut with a knife to make small pieces.

(If you make spätzle a lot, you might find handy a "Spätzle Mill" in a kitchen wares shop. This has an open-bottom hopper that slides over a metal plate with holes in it. Put batter in hopper, and slide back and forth over the water.)

Stir dumplings to keep them from sticking, and cook a few minutes until they float. Remove from water with a slotted spoon, and put in a bowl with a little butter so they don't stick together.

These can be added to a soup or stew directly. If served as a starch with meat and gravy, melt 3 T. butter in a heavy frying pan, and cook until butter begins to brown. Add spätzle, and stir to separate. Stir until warmed through.

Dutch Potatoes and Cabbage

In the Netherlands following a great influx of immigrants from Indonesia and Suriname, Indonesian cuisine has become so popular that it often displaces older traditional fare. It is "something special" that you serve to guests in their honor for festive occasions. Our hosts graciously wanted to do something "nice" for us, but after several days of Indonesian, we asked: "Can you make some traditional Dutch dishes for us?" As a result, we got some delicious sausages (like knockwurst) and this simple and hearty combination.

Simply make mashed potatoes, using three potatoes and lots of butter.

Cut half a small head of green cabbage into small bite-size pieces, and cook in boiling salted water until tender. (You need about 2 cups cooked cabbage.) Drain well.

Mix potatoes and cabbage. Add salt and pepper to taste, and grate a little nutmeg over the top. Serve with buttered rye bread, grilled sausages, and mixed salad or pickled red cabbage for a delicious supper.

Asparagus
(Spargel)

Fresh asparagus, when available, is a favorite vegetable in Germany, Switzerland, and the Netherlands. In some places in Germany, the day the first asparagus of the year is harvested is (or used to be) a holiday.

Take a bunch of fresh asparagus, hold one stalk at each end and snap to see where the tough part ends. Cut the other stalks to that length and discard woody ends. Put tender ends into a steamer (the Chinese bamboo kind works best) over boiling water. Steam for about 8 minutes until the asparagus is tender but still a little firm. Remove from steamer and serve with melted butter.

Strudel

This is a delicious dessert, and is not hard to prepare unless you try to make your own strudel dough, which is basically impossible.

8 to 12 sheets frozen phyllo pastry dough
1 (21 oz.) can apple or other fruit pie filling
½ stick butter, melted
¼ cup raisins (optional)
½ tsp. vanilla (optional)
½ pint whipping cream
1 T. sugar

Thaw phyllo according to package directions. (If the box has 2 separately wrapped rolls, thaw only 1.) Unroll dough and cover with a damp towel so the dough will not dry out (which it does very quickly). Take 2 sheets of phyllo and brush with melted butter. Put 2 more sheets on top of the first ones and brush these with butter. Repeat until you have 8 to 12 sheets (depending on how much crust you like).

Spread filling on lower third of long side of dough. If you are using apple filling, many people like to add raisins and/or vanilla. If using cherry, blueberry, strawberry, etc., filling, the raisins and vanilla are not needed.

Tuck in ends, and starting at filling side roll into a log, loose edge down. Flatten slightly, brush outside with more butter and cut 3 slits in the top to allow steam to escape. Place on cookie sheet and bake in a preheated 350° oven for about 30 minutes or until golden brown. If your oven doesn't cook evenly, rotate the pan about halfway through. When done, allow to cool slightly, and cut into thick slices.

Whip cream and sugar until stiff peaks form, and serve on the side of the strudel. You can use vanilla ice cream in place of or in addition to the whipped cream. This isn't as authentic, but it sure is good.

Dutch Pancakes

Thanks again to Paul Peucker for this Netherlands favorite. Paul says these are "traditionally eaten as a dessert."

For 8 pancakes:

5 T. flour	a little less than a cup of milk, divided
½ tsp. salt	
1 egg	½ stick of butter, divided

Combine flour and salt. Add the egg and stir in half the milk. Keep adding milk until a smooth batter is formed.

Melt ¼ stick of the butter and add it to the batter. Heat the rest of the butter in a skillet and add ⅛ of the batter. Let the batter spread evenly throughout the pan. Cook until upper side is dry and turn it to cook the other side.

Pancakes can be served with sugar, jelly, chocolate paste, or bacon and syrup.

Bad Boll Plum Tart
(Zwetschgenkuchen)

Roy Ledbetter contributed this treat. While serving in Germany in the 1970s, he had this in the town of Bad Boll made with plums they picked from trees at the home of Br. Karl Schmidt, retired treasurer of the Provincial Mission Board. Sr. Schmidt did the baking.

Roy explains that "Zwetschgen" is the South German name for plums (not the High German "Pflaumen"). He also says it is essential to use "the small blue Italian plums." We know them as "damsons."

Crust:

2 cups flour
½ cup sugar
pinch salt
1 tsp. baking powder

¼ lb. butter (very cold, cubed)
1 egg, beaten
1 tsp. vanilla extract
1 to 2 T. ice water

Filling:

2 lbs. blue Italian plums
¾ cup sugar
cinnamon

Glaze:

½ cup apricot preserves
½ cup sugar

Prepare a tart pan with removable bottom by greasing it with cooking spray. Preheat oven to 375°.

Prepare the dough first. Sift together 2 cups flour, ½ cup sugar, pinch salt, and 1 tsp. baking powder. Separately combine egg and vanilla. With pastry knife cut the cubes of butter into the flour. When it resembles fine meal, add egg and vanilla mixture. Then add 1 T. very cold water, and stir mixture into a soft dough. Add additional water by teaspoons if necessary. Form into a thick flat circle (it will be soft). Cover in plastic wrap and chill for at least 1 hour until firm.

In the meantime, cut plums in half and remove and discard stones.

When the pastry is good and firm, flour a board, and roll it out big enough to fit your tart pan. It should be between ⅛ and ¼ inch thick. Cut off overhanging edges, and press dough into flutes of tart pan. Be sure there are no holes, or juice will leak out.

Arrange plum halves on dough in concentric circles, cut side up. Sprinkle plums with sugar and generous shakes of cinnamon. Place tart pan on a baking sheet to catch any drips and bake for 30 minutes at 375°.

While the tart is baking, make glaze by melting apricot preserves in a saucepan with sugar. Remove tart from oven when crust is golden brown. While tart is still hot, use a pastry brush to dab each plum with melted apricot glaze.

Let tart cool in pan before trying to remove the tart bottom from the pan. Serve *"mit Schlag,"* that is, with a dollop of whipped cream alongside each slice.

Strawberry Torte

Most fancy tortes come from a bakery, but you can make a simple one at home with prepared ingredients. This is really a large strawberry shortcake. Thanks again to Roy Ledbetter for his ideas from the Black Forest on assembling the fancier version of this cake and for the "platform" recipe.

> 1 sponge cake round from the supermarket
> 1 (21 oz.) can strawberry pie filling, or 1 quart
>   fresh strawberries and a package of strawberry
>   glaze (or ½ cup strawberry or currant jelly melted
>   with 1 T. sugar as glaze)
> ½ cup strawberry jam
> whipped cream as in strudel recipe (page 38)

Split cake with serrated knife into upper and lower halves. On cut sides of each half, spread a layer of whipped cream. Spread strawberry jam on bottom half, then put the top on, whipped cream side down. Spread top of cake with a thin layer of whipped cream. Then spread filling on top of this (or remove caps of strawberries, slice berries in half and arrange them in a spiral on top of the cake, then cover thinly with glaze). Decorate top with whipped cream dollops. You can also spread whipped cream around the side. Chill, slice, and serve.

Note: You can, of course, bake your sponge cake (or yellow cake) yourself using boxed mix or your favorite recipe. A springform cake pan works best for this. Roy provides a cake recipe for this from the Black Forest:

Königsfeld Sponge Cake

4 eggs
scant ¾ cup sugar

scant ¾ cup sifted flour
1 to 4 T. very warm water

Preheat oven to 350°.

Break eggs into a mixing bowl.

The original recipe says to add 4 T. very warm water and beat briefly until very foamy. I find that that much water keeps the eggs from getting thick enough later (apparently our eggs have more moisture than the German ones). Omit the water for now.

Add 170 grams (scant ¾ cup) of granulated sugar to the eggs, and beat with a mixer until the mass makes very stiff peaks and you can turn the mixing bowl upside down without the eggs falling out. Fold in 170 grams (scant ¾ cup) of sifted flour. (If the mixture is too thick now, add a little water.) Pour into a well-greased 10½-inch springform pan with greased waxed paper cut to fit the bottom and side. Bake at 350° in the middle of a preheated oven for 15 to 20 minutes until the cake is risen and golden brown. Do NOT open the oven while it is baking. Cool for 10 minutes, remove from pan, and finish cooling.

Add filling and assemble as in recipe on previous page.

Sisters' Kisses

Roy Ledbetter says: "I first encountered Sisters' Kisses in Königsfeld, when the late Sister Brigitte Meyer gave me a box of the little sweet meringues that had been baked in the Brethren's House bakery in Christiansfeld in southern Denmark. They seem to have been made in several congregations in the 19th century, most notably Herrnhut. Unlike Moravian mints, these are baked meringues."

We assume the name implies that these little sweets were the closest you were going to come to getting a kiss from the Single Sisters.

> 1 cup sugar
> 7 egg whites
> ½ tsp. peppermint oil

In a double boiler over simmering water beat sugar, egg whites, and peppermint oil to stiff peaks. Cool. Use either a pastry bag with a star tip or 2 teaspoons to make little kisses on a well greased and floured baking sheet. Bake at 275° for 15 minutes or a little more. Do not brown.

You can also add a couple of drops of red food coloring to the mixture before beating so the color is pink like the ribbons on the Single Sisters' traditional caps. This is not original, but seems fitting. Use blue if you prefer Married Sisters.

Note: Roy says: "With the addition of chopped almonds and chopped citron, and omitting the peppermint (and coloring), they become 'Widows' Kisses.'"

Great Britain and Northern Ireland

Moravians first came to England in the 1730s on the way to mission stations elsewhere. Soon, however, English friends formed congregations and spread to several areas of England and into Northern Ireland also.

British cooking often has a bad reputation for being bland and uninteresting. That is unfair, for done well this land's dishes are not only filling, but flavorful and interesting as well. Try the examples below, and see if you agree.

Fresh Tomato Soup

This first dish is an excellent example of British cooking's being far more than expected. Canned tomato soup is a comfort food we all know, but this rises to a whole other dimension. Serve it at a holiday gathering once, and it will become a tradition.

This is called "Fresh Tomato Soup" for a reason. Usually canned tomatoes do as well as fresh ones in cooked dishes. In a pinch, you can use canned tomatoes in this recipe. It will be very good. But in this case fresh is best. For the full glory of this soup, use the best fresh tomatoes you can get even in December.

4 large tomatoes	freshly grated nutmeg
2 T. butter	1 T. plus 1 tsp. sugar
1 onion, diced	2¾ cups chicken broth
2 tsp. garlic, minced	⅓ cup orange juice
½ cup canned carrots, diced	1 cup heavy cream
salt and pepper to taste	mint leaves for garnish

Remove hard core from tomatoes and make a crosswise incision in the other end. Blanch a few minutes in boiling water until skin begins to loosen. Peel off skins (this is the only tedious part) and cut tomatoes into large pieces.

Melt the butter in a large soup pot or Dutch oven and add the onions. Cook 4 to 5 minutes. Then add the tomatoes, garlic, and carrots with some salt and pepper. Cook on medium heat until tomatoes are soft (10 to 15 minutes). Stir often so they do not burn.

Let cool a bit, then puree tomato mixture in a blender. A little texture will remain, but get it mostly smooth. **Note:** Do this in three batches, or the hot mixture will blow the lid off the blender.

Return mixture to pot over medium low heat. Add 6 to 8 grates (about ¼ tsp.) nutmeg and the sugar, and cook for a couple of minutes, stirring well. Add chicken broth and orange juice, and stir. Then pour in cream, and stir until hot (not boiling). (And yes, it's supposed to be orange, not red.) Check for seasoning. Serve in bowls with mint garnish.

If fresh mint is not available, sprinkle some mint (real mint, *not* peppermint) extract over some dried parsley and use that instead. Another alternative is to garnish with basil instead of mint.

This recipe will serve four people, but you may want to double the recipe since your friends and relations will want to take some home.

Compare this with the tomato soup recipe of India (page 209).

Roast Beef and Yorkshire Pudding

This is one of the most famous English dishes, and is great as the centerpiece for a holiday, birthday, or special weekend. The "pudding," of course, has nothing to do with dessert.

Choose a nice sirloin roast of beef. It needs to be at least three pounds to roast well. It will serve way more than four persons, but is wonderful for leftovers and sandwiches. Rub the meat all over with Worcestershire sauce, a little catsup, and salt and pepper. (I like to add garlic too, but that is up to you.) Place on a roasting rack in a large pan with a cup of water in the bottom. Roast in a preheated 350° oven for 20 minutes a pound. This makes the meat medium. Shorten or lengthen the time if you prefer it rare or more done. If the pan is going dry during cooking, add a little more water.

Now for the pudding:

1 cup flour
½ tsp. salt
1 cup milk

¼ cup water
2 eggs

Have the ingredients at room temperature so they will puff during cooking. In a large bowl mix the flour and salt and stir in the milk and water. Beat the eggs in a separate bowl and add to mixture. Stir to mix, then beat with a wire whisk (or rotary or electric mixer) until large bubbles form in the batter. This helps it rise during cooking.

Traditionally, the pudding was cooked in the pan under the beef, but individual puddings work better. Put a pat of butter in each compartment of a regular 12-hole muffin tin. Put in oven until butter is hot and beginning to bubble. Ladle batter equally into each compartment. (Each one will be about two-thirds full.) Place in preheated 350° degree oven and bake until batter has risen and is golden brown. Don't open the oven to check on them for the first 15 minutes, but after that look to see if they are cooking evenly. Rotate the pan if they are not. Cooking time is generally 40 to 45 minutes. If any of them stick, running a thin knife blade around the edge will help get them out.

To serve, slice beef, and give each person one or two puddings to start with. Pour on lots of gravy.

To make the gravy, pour off most of the grease from the roasting pan. Put roasting pan on stovetop and add a T. or so of flour. Cook until flour begins to brown, and add 2 cups beef broth. Stir until thickened, check for seasoning, and enjoy.

Fish and Chips

This is another of those foods everyone thinks of in relation to the British Isles. The light crispy batter goes perfectly with the tender fish. The "chips," of course, are totally unlike American "potato chips."

4 thick filets of cod or haddock (4 to 6 oz. each)	3 T. club soda
1½ cups flour	4 large potatoes
1 tsp. baking soda	oil for frying
½ tsp. salt	salt
¾ cup water (more or less)	malt vinegar

Mix flour, soda, and salt. Pour in about half of the water. Add club soda (which helps the batter puff as it cooks). Mix with a wire whisk. Add more water as needed to make a medium batter, about the consistency of that used for pancakes. Add more water if it is too thick. Add more flour in the unlikely event it is too thin. Let the batter rest at room temperature for at least a half hour. Up to an hour is better.

While batter is resting, peel potatoes and cut them into long strips, about ½ inch wide and thick. Dry them and sprinkle on a little salt.

Heat about 3 inches of oil in a deep pot to about 350°. Fry potatoes in the hot oil until they begin to get a little tender, say 7 to 10 minutes. Remove them from the oil, and let rest 5 minutes. Increase oil temperature a little, then return potatoes to the oil, and fry until light golden brown. Remove, drain, and salt immediately. Keep them in a warm oven while you fry the fish. (Chips keep warm better than fish.)

Reduce oil temperature to 350° again. Dry the fish, salt and pepper it, and dip each piece in batter to coat completely. Let it drip over the bowl for a couple of seconds to remove excess, then carefully lower fish into hot oil. Don't worry if some blobs of batter float off. They make delicious "crunchy bits." Just fish them out when they get golden brown.

Fry the fish until they become golden brown. Turn them in the oil once or twice. This will take 5 to 10 minutes. Remove fish with slotted spoon, drain, and salt immediately.

Serve with "chips," and let each person shake on as much malt vinegar as desired.

(Yes, catsup and tartar sauce are delicious with fish, but they shouldn't go with this!)

Fish Cakes

While living in Oldham we would often pick these up to take home for supper after our weekly excursion to Tommyfield Market.

1 lb. of cooked cod, haddock, etc.	¼ tsp. thyme
1 cup mashed potatoes	salt and pepper
1 egg	breadcrumbs
½ tsp. malt vinegar or lemon juice	

Flake fish into very small pieces. Mix in remaining ingredients (except breadcrumbs) one after the other. If mixture is too sticky to hold together, mix in a few breadcrumbs but don't overdo it.

Form into 8 cakes about 2½ inches across and about ½ inch thick. Roll in breadcrumbs to coat all sides. You can refrigerate these ahead of time. Fry in hot oil until golden brown outside.

Meat Pies

These are great served with chips (page 50) and gravy and malt vinegar. Bites can also be dipped in a little English mustard (hot!). The trick is in the crust, which must be tender but heavy enough to hold its shape when cooked.

For the crust:

3¼ cups flour
½ tsp. salt
½ tsp. sugar
½ cup solid vegetable shortening
½ cup cold water
3 T. milk
1 egg, beaten

Add salt and sugar to flour and mix. Add shortening and rub it evenly into the flour with your fingers. Bring water and milk to a boil and add to flour mixture. Since mixture is now hot, stir at first with a spoon to make a stiff dough. When it has cooled enough to handle, use your hands to finish mixing. If dough is too stiff, add more hot water, 1 T. at a time.

Take off about one-fourth of the dough to make lids for the pies later. Divide the rest of the dough into four equal parts.

For cooking, use a muffin tin designed for four very large muffins. Coat well with non-stick cooking spray. Take a piece of dough and flatten it as much as you can. Put it into one of the compartments and press out to cover bottom and sides, sticking out a little on top. Repeat for each compartment.

Put filling of choice (see suggestions below) into each compartment, nearly to the top.

Take remaining dough, divide it into four, and press and stretch out to make lids. Put one on top of each pie, and crimp edges to seal. Cut a slit or two into each top to let the steam out. Brush with egg beaten with a dollop of water. Bake in a preheated 350° oven until dough is firm and a little brown. (It will not get very dark in color.) This generally takes about 45 minutes. Let cool for 10 minutes, then give the pies a twist to make sure they aren't stuck anywhere. If they are, run a slim knife down the side between the tin and the pie. Place a platter upside down on top of pies and invert muffin tin to release pies. Turn pies right side up on platter.

Filling suggestions: The pies can be filled with leftover chopped up beef and gravy (with or without fried onions and/or mushrooms). Pork can be used also. A "meat and potato pie" has broken up hamburger (about 1 lb.) fried with onions and small cubes of cooked potato. When the meat is almost cooked, sprinkle on salt and pepper and a couple of splashes of Worcestershire sauce. Then sprinkle on 1 T. of flour, stir, and cook a bit. Then add a little broth or water to make a thick sauce around the meat. Another alternative is to layer slices of cheese and onion into the pie to make (you guessed it) "cheese and onion pie." In any case, fill the compartments not quite to the top.

Cornish Pasties

These are simpler to make than the meat pies given above. They originated in Cornwall, where miners found them a handy lunch to take to work. They became popular all over England, often with local names. In the north a similar pasty was called a "Lancashire foot."

⅔ lb. ground beef
1 onion, diced
½ tsp. thyme
salt and pepper to taste

2 tsp. Worcestershire sauce
2 tsp. flour
pie-crust dough

Filling: Crumble ground beef into small pieces and brown in frying pan. Add onion, stir, and cook until it is softened. Add seasonings. If you want, sprinkle on flour and add a little water to bind meat mixture together.

Crust: Use your favorite pie-crust recipe for a covered pie, or use refrigerated pastry from the grocery. Frozen crusts do not work well for this. Roll out pie-crusts to about ¼ inch thick. Cut out four 6- to 7-inch circles or ovals.

Assembly: Place one-fourth of filling on one-half of each circle, and fold and stretch other half over to make a half moon shape. Moisten edges and crimp to seal. Cut slits in top to let steam out.

You can brush the pasties with an egg wash or melted butter if you want a shiny brown finish. Put on baking sheet. Bake in preheated 350° oven until crust is nicely browned (30 minutes or so).

Variation: In the old days, "dessert" was sometimes included in the pasty. Put meat filling on only about two-thirds of lower half of circle. Put a T. or so of fruit pie filling on the rest of that half. Fold dough over as above, and press down to separate meat and fruit. Proceed as above.

Shepherd's Pie

In the British "public" schools this was a staple dish designed to use up leftover meat from the Sunday joint of lamb. You can still do that, but the hamburger version is more common today.

1 to 1½ lbs. ground beef or lamb
1 onion, diced
salt and pepper
parsley, savory, rosemary, etc.
1 T. Worcestershire sauce
½ cup catsup
2 cups mashed potatoes
½ stick butter, melted
paprika (optional)

In a heavy frying pan crumble ground meat and cook with onion. As it browns, add salt and pepper and herbs as desired. When brown, skim out most of the fat and juices. Add Worcestershire sauce and catsup, stir, and cook for 2 or 3 minutes. Turn into an ovenproof pan and spread mashed potatoes on top. Make furrows in the potatoes with a fork. Pour melted butter over the top. You can sprinkle on a couple of dashes of paprika if you like.

Put under broiler until potatoes brown. Spoon out servings.

English mint sauce is good with this. This is fresh chopped mint in malt vinegar and a little sugar. There are commercial varieties, or you can make your own. (Do *not* confuse this with peppermint sauce!)

Lancashire Hot Pot

This Victorian stew became popular all over the country. Original recipes call for kidneys, but since those are not as congenial to our American palates as they are to those of our British friends, I have omitted them. If you want to be absolutely authentic and feel adventurous, get your hands on some lamb kidneys, clean them, slice them up, and throw them in.

1½ lb. lamb, cubed
2 small onions, diced
1 carrot, peeled and sliced
1 cup mushrooms, sliced
4 potatoes, peeled and sliced

1 tsp. thyme
2 cups beef broth (approx.)
1 T. Worcestershire sauce
2 T. tomato paste
salt and pepper to taste

Put a layer of lamb in bottom of ovenproof Dutch oven or deep casserole. Top with a layer of onions, carrots, and mushrooms. Season with salt and pepper and a little of the thyme. Put on a layer of potatoes, and then repeat the process until ingredients are used up, ending with a layer of potatoes. (Peel and slice another one if you need to.)

Heat broth and mix in Worcestershire sauce and tomato paste, and pour over ingredients in casserole.

Cover and bake in a preheated 350° oven for an hour. Check after 30 minutes to make sure there is enough broth remaining. Add a little water if you need to. When the hour is up, uncover casserole, brush potatoes with melted butter, and return to oven uncovered for another 15 to 25 minutes until potatoes have browned nicely.

Irish Stew

This is another of those well-known home cooking or pub fare dishes, this time from Ireland originally. Its enjoyment is not restricted to the Emerald Isle, however.

Since it is similar to Lancashire hot pot (previous page), follow that recipe but omit the carrot, mushrooms, and tomato paste.

Garnish with parsley and serve in large bowls with a good-size piece of soda bread or what we in America call "biscuits." (If you ask for biscuits with the stew in Britain, you will get a "cookie," not to mention some puzzled looks.)

Sole with Parsley Sauce

This makes a nice lunch or supper or a fish course at a more elaborate sit-down dinner. Cod makes a fine substitute if sole is not available.

Select a nice 4- to 6-oz. filet for each person. Poach gently in water seasoned with onion, bay leaf, salt and pepper, and a splash of vinegar. Six to 8 minutes should do it. Remove and drain.

For the sauce, melt 1½ T. butter in a pan, add 1 T. flour, and stir over low heat to make a light roux (don't let it brown). Add 1 cup milk or half-and-half, stirring constantly. Stir in 2 T. dried parsley and salt and pepper to taste. Add a pinch of sugar if you like a mellower sauce.

Sausages

There is nothing like a proper British sausage or "banger." Unfortunately, they have not caught on in most of America. Getting casings and a sausage stuffer to make your own is also a chore. If you have the equipment and supplies, by all means make cased sausages out of this. If not, these will provide at least a pale imitation of the glories of a banger.

1 lb. ground pork or beef	1 tsp. savory
¼ cup finely diced suet or frozen pork fat	½ tsp. freshly grated nutmeg
2 tsp. malt vinegar	¼ tsp. each of sage, rosemary, and thyme
½ cup flour	1 egg
salt and pepper	

If you have a meat grinder, run the ground meat through it to make it a fine grind. If not, chop the ground meat with a knife or put it in a food processor to make it as fine as you can. If you can't find suet, use the pork fat. (Freezing the fat helps with the dicing and makes it act more like suet as it cooks.) Combine all ingredients to make a smooth mixture. (If the song keeps running through your head, add a pinch of parsley also to make it "parsley, sage, rosemary, and. . . .")

Stuff into casings or shape into links or patties and fry over low heat in 2 tsp. oil until cooked through but not very much browned.

Serve with breakfast eggs, or have with chips (page 50) and fried onions, a sprinkling of cooked English peas, gravy, malt vinegar, and (if you are brave) a little English mustard on the side.

Roast Potatoes

These go well with roasts, chops, or chicken. They should be a little crunchy on the outside but almost creamy inside.

Preheat oven to 350°. Put enough vegetable oil in a roasting pan to cover bottom. Put pan in oven to get oil hot.

Use a medium potato for each person. Peel and cut into large pieces, 8 to 12 per potato, depending on size.

Put 3 T. flour into a large zip-top plastic bag. Add salt and pepper, a little onion and/or garlic powder, and a couple of dashes of paprika. Add potatoes and shake to coat pieces. Shake off excess flour as you take potatoes from the bag.

Carefully put potato pieces into hot oil in pan, return to oven, and roast for about an hour. Do not bother them for at least 20 minutes. After that, turn them once in a while to get all sides into oil. If they absorb all the oil, add a little more.

Ploughman's Lunch

This does not involve cooking. Supposedly, it arose as a collection of foodstuffs a farmer could easily carry into the field so as not to have to return home for the midday meal. Today you are more likely to find it in a "pub."

For each person, take 2 oz. or so of Cheddar or other English cheese. Add a sweet onion (pickled is best), 1 T. of chutney or other relish, and a couple of thick slices of buttered crusty bread. If you're feeling extravagant, you might also have a hardboiled egg, a cooked sausage, or (to combine the best of both worlds) a Scotch egg (see next page). You can take bites of each ingredient in whatever combination you please, or slice the cheese, onion, egg, and sausage, and put everything on the bread to make a sandwich.

Scotch Eggs

These make a handy snack or part of an appetizer selection. Their popularity extends far beyond Scotland.

>6 hardboiled eggs
>1 lb. bulk sausage
>1 cup breadcrumbs
>oil for frying

Remove shells from eggs. Cover completely with sausage, then roll in breadcrumbs. Fry in oil until nice and brown all around.

These can be eaten whole, or sliced into halves or quarters, depending on what you are eating them with.

Beans on Toast

This is not elegant, but it makes a tasty breakfast, lunch, or "tea."

Toast 4 pieces of bread on one side under broiler. When they brown as much as you like, take them out, put small pieces of butter on the untoasted side, and place that side up under broiler until brown.

Warm a 16-oz. can of pork and beans in a pot, then divide evenly over toasted bread.

Run back under the broiler for a couple of minutes, with a strip or two of cooked bacon on top. British bacon is between American and Canadian bacon, so use either. For a special treat, add a fried egg.

While the broiler is on, you may also want to cut small tomatoes in half, brush them with oil, salt and pepper, and put them under the broiler until the tops bubble and brown a little. These go well with the beans on toast, egg, etc. A little English mustard on the side gives the dish a kick, but be careful. Remember: it's hot!

Parkin

Parkin is the Lancashire term for a not-too-sweet type of gingerbread. It is great for a snack or at tea time.

1 egg
⅓ cup light brown sugar
⅓ cup warmed dark corn syrup
⅓ cup vegetable oil
1 cup plus 2 T. flour
1 tsp. baking powder
⅓ tsp. baking soda
1 tsp. powdered ginger
½ tsp. ground cinnamon
¼ tsp. ground nutmeg
¼ cup hot water (approx.)

Cream egg and sugar with mixer. Add syrup and oil, and mix well. Add dry ingredients, and mix well again. Add enough water to make a thick batter, and pour into a greased and floured 3 x 9-inch (more or less) loaf pan.

Bake in a preheated 350° oven for 30 minutes. Insert a toothpick or thin knife into the center. If it comes out clean, the parkin is done. If not, cook for a few minutes more, and try again.

Let cool for 10 to 15 minutes. Remove from pan. Let cool about 15 minutes more. Cut off ½-inch slices as you need them.

Trifle

Trifle is a very traditional English dessert. It consists of cake pieces, fruit, custard, and whipped cream. So what's not to like? There are fancy versions featuring raspberries and liqueur (similar to the Italian "tiramisu" but without the coffee). The following version, however, is closer to what we enjoyed with the folks in Lancashire.

12 ladyfingers or pieces of sponge cake
1 large (6 oz.) or 2 3-oz. packages of strawberry gelatin dessert
2 envelopes of English custard powder
6 T. sugar
3 cups milk
1 cup whipping cream
1 T. sugar
"sprinkles"

Cover the bottom of a large bowl with the cake pieces. (A clear bowl works best so the layers of the trifle can be seen.) Mix the gelatin according to package directions and pour over cake. Allow to sit for several hours to set. Prepare custard according to package directions with the sugar and milk. Let custard cool to almost room temperature, then spread it over gelatin and cake. Whip cream with sugar and spread on top of custard. Decorate with "sprinkles."

Note: If you can't find the custard powder you can make your own custard. Heat 3 cups milk (or half-and-half) in double boiler until bubbles form around the edge. (A large bowl on top of a pot of boiling water works fine.) Remove from heat and allow to cool slightly. In another bowl beat 6 eggs with 3 T. sugar, 1½ T. cornstarch, and a pinch of salt. Mix in a few spoonfuls of the milk to "temper" the eggs so they won't curdle when added to the hot milk. Return milk to heat and add egg mixture. Stir constantly until custard thickens. Be patient. This may take 20 minutes. When thick, stir in 1 tsp. vanilla.

Custard Sauce for Tarts

This is a thinner version of the custard above. Poured over your favorite fruit pie, it raises the good to the sublime.

1¼ cup milk
2 eggs
1 T. plus 1 tsp. sugar

1 tsp. cornstarch
pinch of salt

Use these amounts and use the cooking instructions given for the firmer custard above.

Put in a gravy boat and let people pour as much as they like over slices of fruit pie (usually called a "tart" in Britain). Tarts do not really need a top crust if served with custard sauce.

North America

(including Alaska and Labrador)

Moravians first came to what is now the United States in 1735 in Savannah, Georgia. When that settlement did not work out they moved in 1741 to Pennsylvania, where Bethlehem became the headquarters for what came to be the Northern Province. From there the church spread to Ohio, the upper Midwest, and California, and came to have churches in Canada also.

Work in the South began in 1753, and Salem soon became the headquarters of the Southern Province.

Moravian work in Labrador can be traced back to 1764. For 150 years the church owned a series of ships (the "Moravian navy") to supply this station. Moravians came to Alaska in 1884. Though Alaska and Labrador are part of the United States and Canada respectively, they are separate provinces in the Moravian world.

The Northern and Southern Provinces have been enriched by members from the Caribbean and Central America in the last decades. They are certainly American Moravians, but it will be more convenient to deal with the dishes they brought with them when we explore the foods of their homelands.

Since most of our readers are acquainted with "American" cooking in general, we will give only a few especially Moravian or regional recipes here.

Moravian Chicken Pie

This and sugar cake (page 87) are probably the best-known "Moravian" dishes in America, at least in the Southern Province. Their sale is a major fundraising tool also. Indeed, an architect designing a church building project was once told: "Don't give me the cost in dollars. How many chicken pies per square foot are we talking about?"

They are all chicken, broth, and crust — no vegetables — and are very different from "chicken pot pie." Every congregation has its own slightly different way of doing these, but the version given here contains the essentials.

Make 1 batch of your favorite pie-crust recipe for a covered pie. In an emergency you could use commercial refrigerated or frozen ones, but please don't announce that I'm condoning heresy by saying that.

Place a cut-up chicken in a pot with salt, pepper, and water to cover. Boil gently until tender, 30 minutes or so.

Remove chicken from pot and allow to cool enough to handle. Remove skin and take meat off bone. Tear into bite-size pieces and shreds. Taste, and salt and pepper as needed.

Put chicken pieces into rolled-out crust in a pie pan. Sprinkle 1 T. flour over the meat. Then pour about ½ cup chicken broth over it.

Cover with rolled out dough, trim, and crimp edges. Cut a hole in the top to let out steam. Bake in a preheated 350° oven for 45 minutes or until crust is golden brown. Rotate partway through for even cooking.

Make gravy by cooking 1 T. flour in 1 T. melted butter over medium heat for a couple of minutes. Do not let it brown. Stir in approximately 1 cup chicken broth to make a slightly thickened gravy. Taste for salt and pepper. (You can add 2 or 3 shakes of poultry seasoning, but the gravy is good without it.)

Slice pie, pour on gravy, and serve with boiled potatoes, green beans (cooked with a little ham or bacon for flavor), and Moravian slaw, below.

Compare this with the South African version of chicken pie (page 171).

Moravian Slaw

The "official" recipe from the Home Church cookbook says: "Take 60 pounds of cabbage . . . serves 375." The following is a little more manageable.

¼ head green cabbage, grated fine 1 tsp. onion, finely chopped
¼ green pepper, chopped fine 1 T. sweet pickle cubes
1 T. pimento, diced Salt to taste (no pepper)

Combine the above ingredients. A food processor is easier than a box grater to prepare the cabbage.

Dressing: Stir 5 T. vinegar and 2 or 3 T. sugar into 1 cup very warm water. Pour over cabbage and other ingredients, and stir. (Sometimes ¼ tsp. of celery seed is added.)

Let sit in refrigerator for a couple of hours (overnight is better) for flavors to blend. Check again for seasoning, and serve.

Creamed Cabbage

This is a particularly good Pennsylvania version of coleslaw.

Take ¼ head green cabbage (minus tough outside leaves) and slice thin. Add salt and pepper to taste. Mix 4 T. mayonnaise, 4 T. sour cream, 2 tsp. milk, 2 tsp. lemon juice, and 2 tsp. sugar. Pour over cabbage, stir, and let stand to blend flavors.

Warm Bacon Dressing

The Pennsylvania Dutch probably invented this, but Moravians enjoy it too.

Fry three strips of bacon until crisp. Remove bacon. If the bacon doesn't render enough fat, add a little oil to make 2 T. Reduce heat to medium. Add 2 tsp. flour to pan and cook for a few seconds. Add 1 T. brown sugar and 1 T. plus 1 tsp. vinegar. Stir in enough water (¼ cup or so) to make a pourable dressing. It will thicken as it stands, so leave it a little thin at this point. Break a piece or two of the bacon into small pieces and add to dressing. Serve over lettuce. (Munch remaining bacon as a snack, or save it for breakfast or a sandwich.)

Moravian Historical Society
(Nazareth, Pennsylvania)
Annual Meeting Traditional Lunch

This is a medley of Pennsylvania staples. For about 100 years it was served to Society members and guests annually on the day of their business and lecture meetings. After the lapse of a few years, the Society reinstated this gem for its 150th anniversary in 2007. For each four people:

¾ lb. dried beef, sliced thin
¾ lb. boiled ham, sliced thin
1 lb. mild white Cheddar cheese
    in ¾-inch cubes
1 loaf each sliced rye
    and white bread

1 stick butter
2 cups cottage cheese
1 cup apple butter
sugar cake (page 87)
water, coffee, and tea

Place each ingredient on a platter or in a bowl as appropriate. Pass around the table for all to take as much as they like. It is traditional to serve yourself the cottage cheese first and then put apple butter over it.

Chicken and Dumplings

As with chicken pot pie and Moravian chicken pie, there are two very different versions of this. The more usual version throughout the country has vegetables and raised dumplings. The other, more restricted to parts of the South, is basically chicken, broth, seasoning, and cooked dough. The second version tastes much better than it sounds. Dumpling recipes from other lands can be found on pages 12, 180, and 220.

Version A

Thanks to my son, Eric, for the specifics of this version.

3 T. vegetable oil
2 carrots, sliced
1 or 2 ribs of celery, sliced thin
1 medium onion, diced
4 small potatoes, diced
2 T. flour

4 cups chicken broth
2 lbs. cubed chicken
1 tsp. poultry seasoning
salt and pepper to taste
2 bay leaves
dumplings (below)

In a large pot or Dutch oven heat oil and add vegetables. Cook on medium until they begin to get tender, 15 minutes or so. Sprinkle with flour, and cook a few minutes more. Add chicken broth, and stir. When broth is warm, add chicken and seasonings, and cook while you make the dumplings as below.

Dumplings:

2 cups flour
2 T. solid vegetable shortening
¼ tsp. salt

1 tsp. baking powder
1 T. dried parsley
⅔ cup milk (approx.)

Put flour in a bowl and add shortening. Use your fingers to rub the flour and shortening thoroughly together. Add salt and baking powder. Add 1 T. dried parsley. Pour in milk a little at a time and mix to make a medium dough. Drop in large spoonfuls on top of stew. Cook for 10 minutes. Cover, and cook 10 minutes more.

Version B

4 cups chicken broth
salt and pepper to taste
½ tsp. poultry seasoning

½ cup milk (approx.)
1½ cups shredded cooked chicken

Dumplings:

2 cups flour
2 T. solid vegetable shortening
¼ tsp. salt

½ tsp. baking powder
½ to ⅔ cup milk

Bring broth and seasonings to a slow boil as you make dumplings.

Rub shortening into flour with your fingers. Add salt and baking powder. Stir. Mix in milk to make a fairly firm dough.

Roll dough on a floured board to a little less than ¼ inch thick. Cut into 1- by 2½-inch strips, and drop into lightly boiling broth. Cook about 10 minutes until dumplings are almost done.

Add milk and cooked chicken. Stir until heated through (3 or 4 minutes).

Note: Normally the starch from the dumplings will thicken the broth to the consistency of a light cream soup. If it doesn't, make a slurry of 2 tsp. flour and 2 T. water, and stir into broth and dumplings over heat.

Daddy's Meatloaf

Meatloaf is one of the great American comfort foods. Here again, everyone does it differently. Often our favorite version is the one we ate growing up. This is mine.

My father didn't cook until he was drafted in 1944 and was made a "mess sergeant." Not being a professional, he usually did what made sense or smelled right rather than follow the official government recipe. He found he liked to cook and kept doing it when he returned home. He prepared many of our meals. As a child, I thought the neighbors were a strange family, because their mother did all the cooking!

Daddy made many wonderful things, but his meatloaf was always a favorite, and he taught me his way of doing it. Since he never measured anything, for this recipe I had to make the right number of shakes of garlic powder, etc., into a small bowl, and then pour it into a measuring spoon to see how much it was.

2 lbs. hamburger (not the lean kind)
3 slices white bread (end pieces do well)
salt and pepper to taste
½ tsp. onion powder

1 tsp. garlic powder
1¼ tsp. seasoning salt
1 T. Worcestershire sauce
3 eggs, beaten
¾ cup plus 2 T. catsup

Toast bread and tear into small pieces. Soak in a little milk to moisten thoroughly. Then squeeze bread to remove most of the milk.

Add dry seasonings to uncooked hamburger and mix well. Add eggs and Worcestershire sauce, and mix well. Add softened bread and work in thoroughly. Finally mix in catsup, and knead mixture for a minute. **Note:** Catsup goes **into**, not on top of mixture. It will be very moist at this point.

Put mixture into a large glass dish (8 x 12-inch), and shape into a thick loaf, about 4 by 9 inches by 2½ inches high. The large pan lets the fat and extra juices drain away from the meat. Cook in a preheated 350° oven for 1 to 1¼ hours. Top should be brown and crusty, but not burned.

Allow to cool 30 minutes before cutting crosswise into 1-inch slices. This does not really need a gravy, but a mushroom cream sauce is good with it.

Country Style Steak

Along with chicken pie, this is one of the favorite dishes at Moravian gatherings. Do not confuse it with Salisbury steak, which is similar but is made with seasoned ground meat patties.

4 large pieces cubed steak	salt and pepper to taste
3 T. oil for frying	½ cup flour
onion powder	1 (15½ oz.) can beef broth
garlic powder	2 tsp. Worcestershire sauce
seasoned salt	

Sprinkle meat liberally (or conservatively) with seasonings. Shake with flour in plastic zip-top bag to coat evenly. Shake off excess.

Heat oil in large frying pan over medium high heat. Fry meat 4 to 5 minutes a side until flour is browned. Remove meat from pan.

If oil has been absorbed, add a little more to make at least 2 T. Put in a heaping T. of flour (taken from what was left from flouring the meat). Stir a minute or two until flour is light to medium brown. Still stirring, add about ¼ cup of the broth. As it thickens, slowly add the rest of the broth. Stir until gravy is thick and boiling. Reduce heat to medium low. Stir in Worcestershire sauce, add more of the seasonings to taste, and return meat to pan. Let simmer for 5 to 10 minutes. Serve with rice or potatoes and a vegetable. Moravian slaw (page 69) is good with this also.

Chicken Fried Steak

The only "chicken" in this dish is the poultry seasoning, like that for fried chicken. The cream gravy is also like that made for chicken. The meat, however, is all beef.

4 large pieces cubed steak	salt and pepper to taste
3 T. oil for frying	½ cup flour
onion powder	1½ cups milk
poultry seasoning	1 tsp. Worcestershire sauce
seasoned salt	

Sprinkle meat with seasonings. Shake with flour in plastic zip-top bag to coat evenly. Shake off excess.

Heat oil in large frying pan over medium high heat. Fry meat 4 to 5 minutes a side until flour is browned. Remove meat from pan.

Reduce heat to medium. If oil has been absorbed, add a little more to make at least 2 T. Put in a heaping T. of flour (taken from what was left from flouring the meat). Stir for a minute. Do not brown. Still stirring, add about ¼ cup of the milk. As it thickens, slowly add the rest of the milk. Stir until gravy is thick and bubbling. Reduce heat to medium low. Stir in Worcestershire sauce and more of the seasonings to taste. (Some folks like to mellow the gravy with a pinch of sugar at this point.) Return meat to pan. Let simmer for 5 to 10 minutes. Serve with rice and a vegetable.

Partridge (or Chicken) Soup

This recipe is thanks to Judy Nelson, who with her husband, Dan, served in Labrador for a while. This would be a favorite there. Judy in turn got it from Mary Andersen.

The original recipe begins: "Pluck and clean 2 partridges." If you can get partridges, by all means do. Otherwise, a nice stewing hen (cut into pieces) will do.

Cook bird in about 2 quarts water for an hour or so with a small piece of salt beef (check your local Hispanic market; canned corned beef can be substituted).

Add 1 cup chopped cabbage and ½ cup diced turnip or rutabaga. Return to boil. Then add 1 cup rice and 1 small diced onion. Salt and pepper to taste. Cook 20 minutes to half an hour until rice is done.

The original recipe doesn't say how to serve this. You could leave the meat on the bone, or remove skin and bone, tear meat into bite-size pieces, and return to broth.

Caribou Stew

This recipe is derived from one passed on by Judy Nelson from her time in Labrador. For those of us without ready access to caribou, venison is an alternative. And yes, veal or beef can be used also. (Judy says the original form of this recipe was from Elsie Evans.)

2 lbs. cubed caribou
1 cup diced carrots
1 cup diced turnips (or rutabaga)
2 potatoes, diced (optional)
¼ to ½ tsp. garlic powder
1 (1 oz.) envelope onion soup mix
½ cup shredded cabbage
salt and pepper to taste

Cook meat in approximately 2 cups of water until meat is tender (45 minutes or so).

Add carrots, turnips (or rutabaga), potatoes (if used), and cabbage. Stir in garlic powder and onion soup mix, and cook another half hour or so until vegetables are done. Add more water as you go, if necessary.

Labrador Meat Pie

Thanks again to Judy Nelson for passing on this idea from Labrador (from Nellie Winters) on what to do with any leftovers from the caribou stew given above.

Prepare your favorite crust for a covered pie.

Fry some salt pork (or bacon) and remove from pan. Add a diced onion and fry until browned (about 10 minutes). If vegetables from caribou stew are in a large dice, chop them a bit smaller, and add to onion. Do the same with leftover meat, seasoned with a little more salt and pepper. Fry for about 10 minutes, add 2 cups of water, and cook for 10 minutes more. Mix 2 T. flour or cornstarch in ½ cup water, and add to vegetables and meat. Stir until mixture is thickened.

Put hot stew into bottom pie crust. Cover with remaining crust, cut a slit in the top to let out steam, and bake for about 30 minutes until crust is nicely browned.

Chipped Beef on Toast

Generations have grown up without ever tasting this former favorite. That is because the military version in the 1940s (made with powdered milk, etc.) was so bad that returning service people refused to allow it in their homes. Most of their children and grandchildren, therefore, did not have it either. It is time to bring it back.

1 small (2¼-3 oz.) jar dried beef
2 T. butter
2 T. flour
8 slices of toast
1 cup cream
1 cup milk
black pepper to taste

Separate slices of beef and rinse under running water to remove excess salt. Pat dry. Cut slices in half, and then cross wise into about ¼-inch strips.

Melt butter in large frying pan over medium heat. Stir in flour and cook for a minute. Do not brown. Stir in part of cream, and add more cream and milk as gravy thickens. (You can use half-and-half, of course.) Add pepper to taste. Use a good bit of pepper, but *no* salt. The dried beef has plenty. Stir in dried beef, cook for a minute, and serve over toast.

Alaska Sourdough Pancakes

When we hear of sourdough, we usually think of San Francisco, but Fran Huetter, who now lives in Winston-Salem, recalls this as a favorite from her years of service in Alaska.

First you need to make your sourdough starter. There are many recipes for this in numerous cookbooks, but they generally call for equal parts of flour and water, a ¼-oz. package of dry yeast, a couple T. of sugar, and sometimes a little salt. Cover, put in a warm place, stir occasionally, and wait a couple of days. Fran notes that if you are out in "the bush" and have no yeast, you can wait for natural yeasts to work. Add more sugar and salt, and wait two or three more days.

As you use the starter, always save a cup or so, add more flour, sugar, and water, and store it in the refrigerator. "Feed" it with a little flour and sugar every few days, and it can keep going for months or even years.

To make pancakes, add a couple of cups each of flour and water, 1 T. sugar, and a little salt to starter the night before you want to make them. In the morning, remember to save some of the starter for future use, but take enough to make your pancake batter. To the batter add 2 T. sugar, more salt, 3 T. shortening, and an egg, and mix well. A teaspoon of baking soda dissolved in a little water gently mixed in also helps the batter rise.

Cook pancakes on a buttered grill or in a pan. When bubbles appear on top, it is time to turn the pancakes to brown lightly on the other side. Serve with butter, and syrup or honey or jam.

Sourdough can also be used in place of yeast to make muffins, bread, etc. Just remember that it works slower than commercial "quick rise" yeasts.

Salmon Spread

When I asked Fran Huetter if she had any recipes from Alaska, she got with some friends now living in Wisconsin who had served there also, and they sent several selections from a Bethel, Alaska, cookbook containing recipes from Moravians there. Thanks are due to Gert Trodahl, Karen Fluegel, Mickey (May Jane Moser) Romer, and Connie Sautebin.

Interestingly, a couple of the recipes they sent from Wisconsin to North Carolina were from a Nicaraguan Moravian who studied in the Moravian Seminary in Bethel. Only in the Moravian Church!

The following is a representative derivation of the original.

Take about a lb. of leftover salmon (or canned) and mix in salt and pepper to taste, about ¼ cup diced onion, ¼ cup diced celery, 1 or 2 T. pickle relish, and enough mayonnaise to make a spread. Serve on bread or crackers.

Baked Berry Dessert

This is another recipe derived from those sent by the "Alaskan" Sisters in Wisconsin.

Melt about ¾ cup butter in a 9-inch iron skillet. Add a good layer (about a couple of cups) of cranberries or other berries as available. Sprinkle well with equal parts of sugar and chopped pecans.

Make a batter of 2 eggs, a half stick of melted butter (not too hot), ¾ cup sugar, and 1 cup flour, plus a tsp. of baking powder. Pour over berries and bake in a 350° oven for about 45 minutes or until nicely browned.

Labrador Buns
(Mrs. Winter's "Day" Buns)

From Alaska, we return to Labrador. Judy Nelson reports that these are what they use for lovefeasts there. The original recipe makes 60 small buns. I have trimmed it to make about a dozen. However, if you want to serve a whole congregation, multiply by five or whatever you need.

1 (¼ oz.) pkg. dry yeast
2 cups flour
⅓ cup sugar
½ tsp. salt

scant ¼ cup margarine
¾ cup water (approx.)
½ cup raisins

Dissolve the yeast in a little water with a pinch of sugar. Let it "proof" while you combine the rest of the ingredients.

Mix the flour, sugar, and salt. With your fingers, rub the margarine into the dry ingredients until it is well distributed throughout.

Work in yeast mixture and enough water to make a medium soft dough. Add raisins and mix evenly throughout dough.

Put in a warm dark place to rise until doubled.

Punch down, and divide into about a dozen buns. Let stand to rise again.

Bake on a cookie sheet in a preheated 350° oven for about a half hour or until nicely browned.

Chocolate Pie

Chocolate pie is a real favorite at church fellowship suppers. Some people even go to the dessert table first, knowing that if they stop to get the rest of their food, there might not be any chocolate pie left. The following is a deluxe deep-dish version. You can make two thinner pies with the recipe.

Let a deep dish pie crust come to room temperature, and "dock" it by making small holes all over the bottom with a fork. This keeps it from puffing too much during the first cooking. Bake empty crust in a preheated 350° oven until light brown, about 15 to 18 minutes, but keep an eye on it. Remove crust from oven, and increase temperature to 400°.

3 eggs, separated
1¼ cups sugar, divided
6 T. cocoa
3 cups undiluted evaporated milk

¼ tsp. salt, heaping
1 T. butter
1 tsp. vanilla

Cook beaten egg yolks, 1 cup sugar, cocoa, milk, and salt in a pot over medium heat. Stir constantly with a whisk or slotted spoon to keep bottom from burning. When mixture is thick and bubbling (15 to 20 minutes) remove from heat and stir in butter until it melts. Stir in vanilla.

Meringue: Beat egg whites until frothy. Gradually add ¼ cup sugar as you continue beating until stiff peaks form.

Pour chocolate mixture into baked pie shell. (For deep-dish version, you may have a little left over. Put it in a bowl and eat it as pudding.) Spread meringue over top. Make pretty peaks and swirls in it, and bake for 5 minutes until peaks of meringue are golden. You need to keep an eye on this — it burns quickly.

Fudge Pie

This is from Grace Robinson. She got this recipe in 1954 from two non-Moravian "maiden ladies" who ran a boarding house at a South Carolina beach. Moravians have been eating it happily ever since.

1 stick butter	1 cup sugar
2 (1 oz.) squares unsweetened baking chocolate	1 egg
	1 tsp. vanilla
⅓ cup flour	⅛ tsp. (pinch) salt

Preheat oven to 350°. Melt butter and chocolate and cool a little. Add rest of ingredients and mix well. Pour into a greased pie pan (no crust!) and bake 20 to 25 minutes.

The pie is very rich, so small slices are advised. (You can always get another.) It is great cold. It is also great warm. If you serve it warm, a scoop of vanilla ice cream on the side makes it unbelievably good.

You can substitute 5⅓ T. cocoa and another T. of melted butter for the baking chocolate squares. Just mix cocoa and 1 T. butter, then add to remaining ingredients.

Sugar Cake

Again, there are variations to this popular dish, but the following will be pretty close to what most folks think of.

1 cup hot mashed potatoes
1 (¼ oz.) pkg. dry yeast
1 cup sugar
¾ cup butter and solid
    shortening (half of each)

1 tsp. salt
2 eggs, beaten
4 cups flour (approx.)

For topping:

1 lb. box light brown sugar
1 stick or more butter
ground cinnamon

ground nutmeg (optional)
evaporated milk (optional)

Combine potatoes, sugar, butter, shortening, and salt. Stir in yeast and let set in a warm place for a half hour (until the mixture is "spongy").

Stir in beaten eggs and enough of the flour to make a soft dough. Place dough into a bowl and let set for 5 hours or overnight.

Punch down, divide in half, and spread evenly into two 9 x 13-inch greased pans. Let dough rise again. (It won't take nearly as long this time.)

With your finger punch holes all over the top and put a little piece of butter in each. Sprinkle brown sugar and cinnamon (and nutmeg if you use it) into each hole and then all over the top.

Bake in preheated 350° to 375° oven for 20 to 25 minutes. Halfway through, put bottom pan on top, and the top one on the bottom. The sugar will be crunchy. If you like the topping softer (and that seems to be the most popular), sprinkle top liberally with evaporated milk when you rotate pans. (This recipe obviously serves more than four — at least at one sitting.)

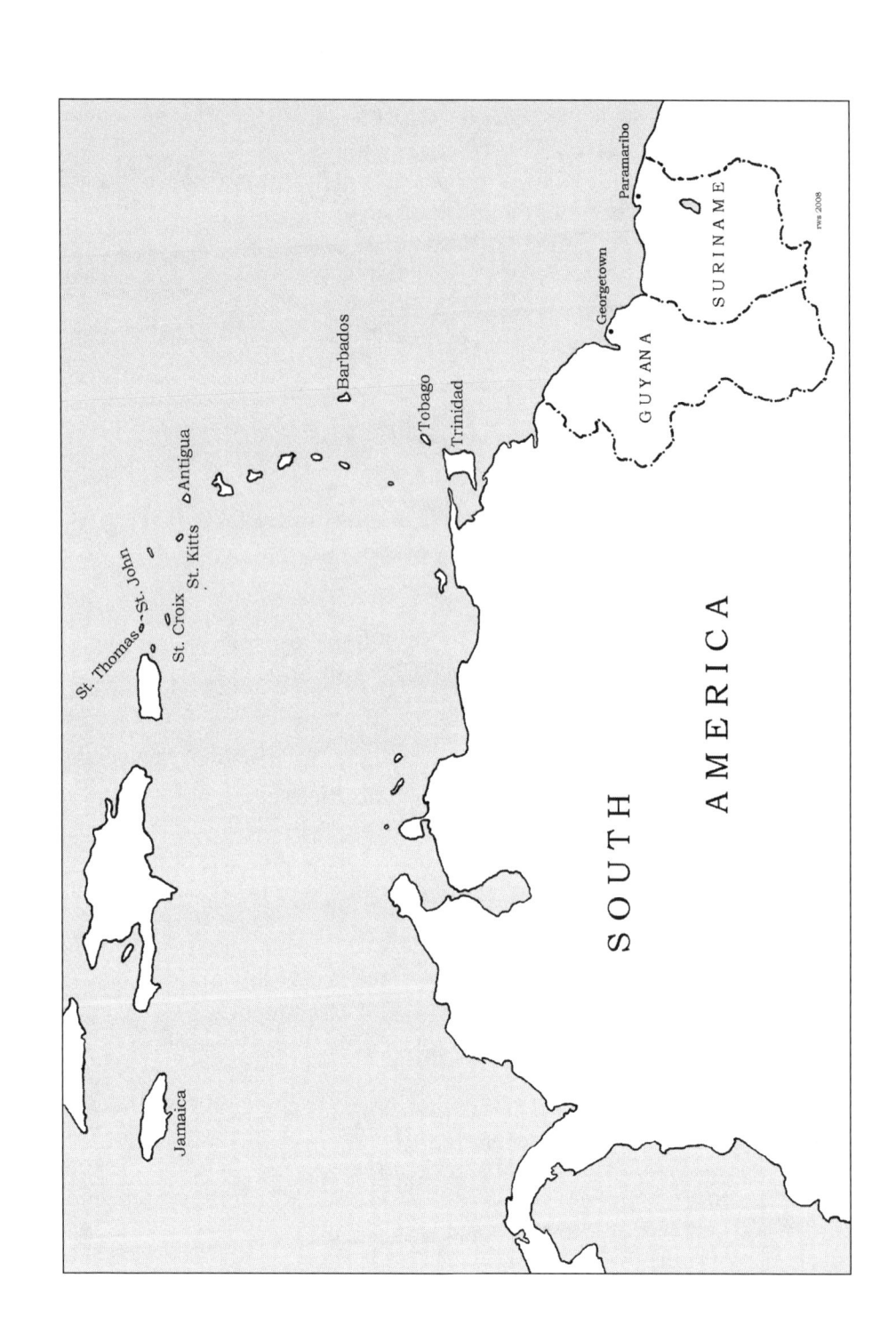

Caribbean Islands and Guyana

Moravian missions began on the island of St. Thomas in 1732. Gradually the work spread to St. Croix and St. John (forming the Virgin Islands), Antigua, Barbados, St. Kitts, and Trinidad and Tobago. These now form the Eastern West Indies Province of the Unity. Since 1754 there has also been a large Moravian presence in Jamaica, which is a separate Province. Guyana (1878) is on the north coast of South America, but has strong cultural links to the island provinces.

In recent decades, many Brothers and Sisters have moved from the islands to the continental United States and Canada. As their presence has enriched the ministry and life of the Northern and Southern Provinces, so the foods they brought with them have enriched our tables.

Fried Plantains

Plantains are now widely available. They look like big bananas, and the inside is like a firm, starchy banana (almost a cross between a banana and a potato). They must be cooked. When ripe the skins turn black.

> 2 fairly ripe plantains
> 2 T. butter
> salt to taste

Peel the plantains and cut in half lengthwise. Cut the halves crosswise into two or three pieces. Fry in butter until they are golden brown all over. Remove from pan, and drain. Some think that a very light sprinkling of salt brings out the flavor.

Serve as a snack or side dish with meat or fish. Add powdered sugar and you have a dessert.

A version from Puerto Rico using green plantains has become very popular recently. Peel two green plantains and cut into 1-inch rounds. In a heavy skillet heat vegetable oil to cover the bottom to about ¼ inch. Fry until plantains are light gold on all sides. Remove from oil and drain. Use two flat hard surfaces to flatten the rounds to about ¼ inch thick. Return to oil and fry again until golden brown. Turn them once, remove, drain, and serve.

Foo Foo

This seems to have originated on Trinidad or Barbados, but it has been known to make an appearance at church suppers in the Virgin Islands too.

>2 green plantains
>water for boiling (no salt)
>salt to taste

Cook plantains in their jackets in boiling water until tender (about 30 to 40 minutes). Remove from water, and let cool enough to handle. Remove peels, and chop plantains. Traditionally the pieces are pounded in a mortar with a pestle to make a smooth paste. If you don't have one, you can mash them with a fork for a long time. Alternatively, puree in a food processor (but don't over-process or you get cement). Add a little water (about ¼ to ⅓ cup) as you blend.

Season with salt, and roll into small balls (walnut size). Serve warm like dumplings with callaloo (page 92) or other soups.

Callaloo

Callaloo (in all its varied spellings) is a favorite soup on many of the islands. As might be expected, local versions vary considerably. The following gives a good idea of what they are all about.

The name comes from the leaves of several wild tropical plants. Fortunately, I have been assured that fresh spinach, Swiss chard, or kale makes a fine substitute.

⅓ cup diced fat ham or salt pork
½ medium onion, diced
1 tsp. garlic, minced
½ lb. spinach, Swiss chard, or kale
¼ tsp. thyme
1 bay leaf

4 cups chicken broth
8 okras
1 lb. crabmeat, small shrimp, or any white fish
salt and pepper to taste
hot sauce to taste

In a large soup pot or Dutch oven, cook ham or salt pork until fat has rendered out. Add vegetable oil if needed to make 2 T. Add onion and cook until soft but not brown. Add garlic and stir quickly. Roughly chop and add greens, and stir for a couple of minutes to coat. Add thyme, bay leaf, and chicken broth. Cut okras into ½-inch pieces and add to hot broth. Cook for about 12 minutes until okra is tender. Add seafood (cut fish into 1-inch pieces) and cook about 4 minutes more. Add salt and pepper and hot sauce to taste. Remove bay leaf before serving.

Some versions replace part of the chicken broth with coconut milk. Many add sliced scallions to broth, or use as garnish. Chives can also be used as garnish.

Pepper Pot Soup

This is a Jamaican specialty that tastes as good in New York City as it does in Kingston. There is a "pepper pot stew" popular in Guyana and the southern islands, but this is different.

½ lb. cubed stewing beef
¼ lb. cubed corned beef
4 cups water
1 lb. mixed spinach, kale, or
    collards, chopped
½ cup onion, chopped
1 tsp. garlic, minced
2 green onions in ¼-inch slices
¼ tsp. thyme

8 slices peeled taro
8 slices peeled yam
6 okras, sliced
1½ tsp. butter
salt and pepper to taste
½ cup cocktail shrimp
½ cup coconut milk
green hot sauce to taste

Simmer meats in 3 cups water in a Dutch oven until beef is tender (45 minutes or so). In a separate pot, simmer greens in 1 cup water until tender (20 minutes or so). Puree the greens with their water in an electric blender. Add to meat pot. Add onions, garlic, thyme, taro, and yam. (If you can't find taro, use a potato; and for the yam, use real white yam, not southern U.S. sweet potato unless you have to.) Simmer until vegetables are tender. Fry the okra in butter, and then add to pot. Add shrimp and coconut milk and heat through. Add hot sauce and salt and pepper to taste.

Salt Fish

Fresh fish are plentiful in the islands. In the days before refrigeration, however, if you needed to keep extra supplies, salting was the way to go. That is no longer necessary, but people still like the flavor and texture of salted fish.

Salt cod is readily available, especially in Hispanic markets. Wash excess salt off, then soak the fish in cold water for about a day. Change the water three times.

The fish can be floured or rolled in cornmeal and fried, or made into fried fish cakes with mashed potatoes, eggs, and seasonings (no salt). Fritters are especially good. In Jamaica, these are called "stamp and go."

½ lb. salt cod
1 cup flour
1 tsp. baking powder
1 egg, beaten
¾ cup milk

1 T. butter, melted
½ onion, finely chopped
chopped hot pepper to taste
oil for frying

Some recipes call for the addition of a little "annatto" coloring. This is made by soaking annatto seeds (available in Latin markets) in hot water or oil to get a strong yellow coloring agent. You may also find commercially prepared versions in those markets.

Soak cod as directed above. Boil in fresh water until fish is flaky (15 minutes or so). Flake the fish, checking to remove any bones, etc.

Mix flour and baking powder. Add egg, milk, and butter. Stir in the coloring if you are using it. Then add onion, pepper, and fish. Mix well. Roll into walnut-size balls. If mixture is too soft to hold its shape, add a little more flour.

Drop into hot oil. Cook a few minutes until balls are golden brown. Drain and serve. These will serve 8 or 10 as appetizers.

Fish Pudding

This seems to have originated on St. Croix in the Virgin Islands. The original called for fresh sea bass, etc., but I find it easier (and more affordable) to use canned mackerel. Canned salmon works too.

1 lb. canned mackerel or salmon
½ medium onion, diced fine
2 eggs, separated
2 T. butter, melted
1 T. lime or lemon juice
½ cup breadcrumbs
salt and pepper to taste
paprika

Drain fish, remove large bones, and work into very small pieces, almost a paste. Mix in onion. Add egg yolks, butter, and juice. Mix well. Stir in breadcrumbs and salt and pepper. (Some folks like to add a splash or two of hot sauce.) Beat egg whites to form stiff peaks, and fold into mixture.

You can put this in a buttered ovenware dish, sprinkle top with paprika, and bake at preheated 350° for about a half hour. When center is firm and top is brown, the dish is done.

If you feel creative, put mixture onto a greased baking sheet, and press into the shape of a fish, with suggestion of fins and gills and cross marks for scales. Sprinkle with paprika, and bake as above. Don't let the thinner "fins" get too dark.

A sauce made of melted butter, salt, and lemon juice to taste is traditional with this dish. You can also add a few shakes of curry powder to the sauce if you like.

Rubs and Marinades

These basic seasoning mixtures can be used to coat or marinate various meats, chicken, and fish to make numerous roasts or stews or grills with an island flavor. Just use these in place of the usual seasonings, marinades, or barbecue sauces in your own recipes. Save leftover rubs and marinades (which haven't come into contact with meats, etc.) to use another time.

A. Dry Rub

Mix together 1 tsp. of each:

salt	oregano
black pepper	garlic powder
brown sugar	ground dry ginger
ground coriander	onion powder

Add ¼ tsp. ground allspice, ½ tsp. ground cumin, and ¼ to 1 tsp. red pepper flakes (depending on how hot you want it). Some people like to add ¼ tsp. curry powder also.

B. "Season Up" Marinade

Mix together:

1 T. malt vinegar	1 T. garlic, minced
3 T. soy sauce	½ tsp. dry oregano (optional)
1 T. Worcestershire sauce	½ tsp. celery seed (or 2
1 T. lime juice	celery leaves, chopped)
½ onion, finely grated	2 T. chives, chopped

Add as much cayenne pepper or hot sauce as you like. That may be only a pinch or a few drops, up to ½ tsp. or more.

C. Jerk Sauce

This Jamaican barbecue sauce or marinade has become popular all over. The original is extremely hot. One recipe I saw called for 10 habañero peppers. Since habañeros are five times or more hotter than jalapeños, I can't imagine what this would do to your mouth. The following is considerably tamer, but make it as hot as you like. (Only consider your family's and your guests' sensibilities.)

¼ cup lime juice
1 T. vinegar
1 T. orange juice
1 green onion, chopped in pieces
1 tsp. ground allspice
1½ tsp. basil, chopped
1 T. brown sugar

½ tsp. ground cloves
1 tsp. dried mustard
1½ tsp. ground thyme
½ tsp. garlic powder
½ tsp. salt
½ tsp. black pepper

Combine above ingredients and puree in blender until fairly smooth.

Now for the hot pepper part: If you want really authentic (and hot) sauce, wear rubber gloves and seed a habañero pepper, chop, add to marinade, and puree again. In place of the habañero, you can use one or two jalapeños or serranos. An easier way is to add habañero hot sauce (or regular hot sauce if you don't have the other). Start with a few drops for the timid (like me). Continue to add pepper sauce a little at a time until the mixture is as hot as you can stand (or can reasonably enjoy).

Curried Goat

Time was, we had to substitute lamb for goat meat in this island favorite. That is still an option, though frowned on by purists. Nowadays goat or kid is more widely available in Hispanic or other ethnic markets, so you may want to try the real thing. Cooked this way, it is much mellower than you may expect. You can also use pork for a similar dish.

2 lbs. goat, etc.
2 T. curry powder
1 jalapeño
1 T. minced garlic
salt and pepper to taste
3 T. oil for frying

1 onion, diced
2 to 3 cups beef, chicken, or vegetable broth
1 bay leaf
½ cup coconut milk (optional)
1 T. lime juice

Cut meat into cubes as for stew. Put into a zip-top plastic bag with the curry, hot pepper (sliced), garlic, and black pepper. Let marinate for several hours.

Remove meat from bag, save any juices, and pat meat dry. Heat oil in a Dutch oven, and cook meat until it is brown on all sides. Remove meat, and cook onions in oil until tender but not brown. Add liquid (if any) from the marinade (take out the hot pepper if you wish), broth, and bay leaf to pot. Heat, and return meat to pot also. Simmer until meat is tender (45 minutes to an hour, depending on the meat). Some like to add coconut milk at the end of the cooking. Stir in the lime juice, remove bay leaf, and serve over rice.

Fungi
(Cornmeal Mush)

This is Caribbean polenta. It is a very popular side dish. For four people, simply stir 1 cup cornmeal into 2 cups salted boiling water. Stir pretty continuously with a whisk for 5 or 6 minutes, breaking up any clumps. Add 1 T. butter, and stir some more. Remove from heat, cover, and let sit for about 5 minutes. Stir and serve.

In the Virgin Islands particularly, sweetened fungi is a popular dessert. Just treat it like your favorite hot breakfast cereal and add more butter, some sugar, and a good splash of milk or cream to taste. A dash of cinnamon is often added too. Stir all together, serve, and enjoy.

Compare this recipe with South Africa's pap, page 180, and Tanzania's ugali, page 187.

Roti

This and the next four recipes are adapted from ones graciously contributed by Mitzi Kimball, who served with her husband, Roger, for many years in Guyana and the Virgin Islands.

In most of the world "roti" refers to flatbreads like Indian chapatti or flour tortillas. This Caribbean raised version is more like a delicious fried biscuit.

> 2 cups self-rising flour
> 2 T. margarine
> pinch of salt
> water to mix (about 1 cup)

Rub margarine into flour, then add salt and some of the water. Mix into a fairly firm dough, adding more water as needed. Let sit for 10 minutes. Divide into 8 pieces, drizzle a little vegetable oil on each, and roll out flat (about ½ inch thick). Leave again for 15 minutes. Cook in lightly oiled frying pan until light brown on both sides.

Mitzi adds: "This serves as a form of bread and is a popular addition to a meal of curried chicken or goat in Guyana in South America."

Johnny Cake

Mitzi Kimball says: "Although not a 'cake,' this bread-like food is delicious with fried fish or fried chicken in the Virgin Islands."

The original recipe calls for 4 cups flour, etc. For our purposes here, a half recipe will do. You can easily double it if you are feeding a large crowd.

2 cups self-rising flour
6 T. sugar
salt to taste
3 T. solid vegetable shortening

1 T. vegetable oil
1 egg, beaten
about ½ cup water

Mix flour, sugar, and salt. Rub shortening evenly into the dry ingredients. Add oil, egg, and just enough water to make a fairly firm dough. Divide into 12 balls. Flatten balls a bit, and fry in more oil over medium-low heat until golden brown (about 5 to 6 minutes). Turn with spatula to brown all around. Check one to make sure the inside is done. If not, return to oil and fry a little longer.

Guava Cheese

Wash, peel, and rub ripe guavas through a sieve. Add 1 cup sugar for every cup of guava pulp. Boil until mixture is thick and begins to shrink from the sides of the pan, stirring continuously. Test a little in cold water; if it forms a ball, pour the mixture into a greased dish. If not, cook some more. When it is firm, cut in squares and toss in fine white sugar.

Note: You may find guava paste in a Hispanic or other market. This eliminates the washing, peeling, and sieving. If the paste is also sweetened, all you have to do is cut it and roll it in sugar.

Mango Sombal

2 very green mangos	sugar, salt, hot pepper to taste
1 onion	1 (15 oz.) can coconut milk

Peel and grate mangos and onion. Add salt, sugar, and hot pepper to taste. Mix well. Add enough coconut milk to make it quite moist. Keep in refrigerator. Make only enough for the day. If there is any left over, it can be kept in the refrigerator, but it is not advisable to eat after the third day.

Lovefeast Ginger Beer (non-alcoholic)

In the warm tropics, fruit punch or ginger beer is preferred to hot coffee or tea for Moravian lovefeasts.

This is Mitzi Kimball's recipe as she gave it to me. It will serve a good-size congregation.

5 lbs. raw ginger
3 to 4 dozen limes

20 to 25 lbs. sugar
a bit of rose water

Grate ginger. Pour hot water over it to cover. Let soak overnight or for about 8 hours. When ginger is released, add the juice from the limes and sugar to taste. Add rose water.

Mitzi adds: "Although served at room temperature or over ice, this lovefeast drink is HOT from the ginger, but it is quite refreshing and delicious. A congregation can be sure that the singing will improve after drinking ginger beer because it 'opens up the pipes.'"

Note: For those of us not planning to serve a lovefeast to an entire West Indian congregation, the following amounts may be more practical:

8 oz. raw ginger
4 or 5 limes
1 gallon of water (heated)

2 to 2½ lbs. sugar
dash of rose water

Scrape off most of the brown skin of the ginger with the back of a spoon or knife. Grate peeled ginger, put it in a large bowl, and pour hot water over it. Let sit for 8 hours. Strain out ginger pieces, add lime juice, sugar, and rose water, and mix well. (Rose water can be found in Indian markets.)

Caribbean Punch

The ladies of Memorial Church on St. Thomas welcomed us with a punch like this. Variations are legion. Use approximately the following proportion of juices. If your can or bottle has a few ounces more or less, the result is still delicious.

3 cups guava nectar
4 cups pear nectar
5 cups pineapple juice

5 cups unsweetened orange juice
4 cups papaya juice or nectar

Mix all ingredients in a very large punch bowl or plastic bucket. Some folks also like to add 2 or 3 cups of grapefruit juice, but I like it better without.

The recipe the Sisters gave me (no amounts included) made a golden brew, but what they served us was red. Using red papaya nectar helped, but it still wasn't really red. Finally, one of the Sisters confessed to the addition of about a half gallon of a popular brand name red tropical punch to help the color (so that is what we do).

Coconut Pie

When we hear "coconut pie" we usually think of a lot of custard and meringue with a sprinkling of coconut. In the islands, when they say "coconut pie," they mean *coconut* pie.

This is a favorite to serve ministers when they come to visit. I cut short many a planned series of shut-in visits, not because of time or heat, but because I simply couldn't hold another piece of delicious coconut pie.

1 deep dish pie shell, unbaked	¾ cup coconut milk
½ cup sugar	2 T. butter, melted
3 eggs, beaten	2 cups shredded coconut
¾ cup evaporated milk	

Cream sugar and eggs with mixer. Add evaporated and coconut milks and butter, and mix well. Rub coconut through your fingers to break up any lumps, and stir into mixture. Pour into pie shell.

Bake in preheated 350° oven until filling is set and pie shell is light brown (about 45 to 50 minutes). Rotate pie halfway through for even cooking.

Mango Pie

Desserts are as popular in the Caribbean as anywhere else. In addition to the coconut pie given above, large homemade thick layer cakes with lots of icing are great favorites. Chocolate, butter crème, and coconut are popular frostings, not really that different from what one finds in the continental U.S.A., but really rich and good. Here is a simple pie with more of a tropical twist.

Take your favorite uncooked pie crust for a 9- or 10-inch pie pan, prick with a fork, and bake for 20 minutes or so until nicely brown.

For the filling, you can use flesh from 2 or 3 fresh mangoes removed from seed, peeled, and pureed. Or take 2 15-oz. cans of mango, drain (reserving a half cup of liquid). Save out a couple pieces cut into strips for decoration, and puree the rest with the reserved liquid.

In sauce pot cook pureed mango, 2 T. lemon or lime juice, and ½ to ¾ cup sugar with 2 T. cornstarch (first dissolved in a little water) until mixture is very thick and bubbly. If mixture doesn't get thick enough, whisk in some more dissolved cornstarch a little at a time. At the end, whisk in 1 T. of butter for added richness.

Pour into baked pie shell, decorate top with reserved mango slices and refrigerate until set (at least 3 hours or overnight), and serve as is, or decorate top with dollops of whipped cream.

An even quicker and easier way is to cook until thick and bubbly 2 cups fruit nectar, ½ cup sugar, 1 T. lime or lemon juice, 3 T. cornstarch dissolved in a little water, and 1 T. butter.

Note: You can also do a similar pie using guava (a personal favorite) or papaya instead of mango.

Suriname

Moravians have been active in Suriname since 1738. This country on the north coast of South America has a remarkably diverse population and cultural history. First there were the Arawaks and other native peoples. Then the Dutch, who controlled the area for centuries, brought in enslaved persons from West Africa. Immigrants from Indonesia, another area long under Dutch control, moved in, and many workers from India and China came also.

All these various heritages are wonderfully reflected in Surinamese cooking. We also note that Moravians and others who went to the Netherlands from Suriname (and others from Indonesia itself) took their Indonesian dishes with them. These foods became so popular there that in the Netherlands, Indonesian cuisine has almost supplanted traditional Dutch fare for festive occasions.

Spicy Peanut Sauce

This is an Indonesian contribution to Surinamese cuisine. It is widely used in countless variations. The following is representative.

½ cup peanut butter (smooth or chunky)
1 tsp. vinegar or lemon juice or lime juice
¼ cup chicken broth
½ to 1 tsp. dried red chili flakes

In a small saucepan, heat all ingredients, and stir until hot and blended.

Add more or less chili flakes depending on how hot you want it. Hotter is traditional, but less hot is fine too. Serve as a sauce over grilled meats, chicken, or fish, or blend into cooked rice or vegetables.

Javanese Chicken Soup
(Saoto)

This comes from Indonesia originally, but has been widely adopted (and adapted) throughout Suriname.

6 cups chicken broth
1 boneless, skinless chicken breast
1 tsp. garlic, chopped
¼ cup onion, chopped
1 bay leaf
¼ cup lemon grass or 3 T. lemon juice
1 hot pepper or dashes of hot sauce
3 T. or more oil for frying
4 oz. vermicelli
½ cup spinach or kale
½ cup bean sprouts
1 tsp. soy sauce
salt and pepper to taste

Bring broth to boil with half of the garlic and onion, and the bay leaf, lemon grass (or juice), hot pepper, and salt and pepper to taste. Simmer for 10 minutes to flavor broth, then strain to remove solids. Slice chicken thin and add to broth. Cook 6 or 7 minutes until chicken is done. Remove chicken from broth and set both aside.

Break vermicelli (or other thin pasta) into 2- or 3-inch pieces. Fry in oil until lightly browned. Remove pasta from oil, add it to the broth, and boil about 12 minutes until pasta is tender. As pasta cooks, fry rest of onion and garlic in remaining oil and set aside.

Divide uncooked greens and bean sprouts equally into 4 bowls. Do the same with the chicken. With a slotted spoon remove pasta from broth and put in bowls also.

Bring broth to a full rolling boil. Ladle very hot broth over mixture in bowls (it will quickly cook the greens and bean sprouts). Season with soy sauce, add more hot sauce if you wish. Garnish with the fried onions and garlic.

Meat and Cassava Soup

This soup came from West Africa originally and was adapted to local conditions. It also can be made hotter or milder as desired.

1 lb. beef or lamb
1 lb. cassava (yucca), peeled and cubed
4 cups beef broth
2 stalks celery
1 small onion
½ tsp. marjoram
1 hot pepper (more or less)
salt and pepper to taste
2 cups coconut milk

Cut meat into cubes and cook with cassava pieces in broth for about 10 minutes. Add celery and onion cut into bite-size pieces. Add marjoram, hot pepper (or pepper sauce), and salt and pepper to taste. Cook until cassava is tender (about 30 minutes).

Add coconut milk, reduce heat, and simmer for another 5 or 10 minutes. Check for seasoning, and serve.

Note: If cassavas (called yuccas in Hispanic markets) are not available, you can use potatoes instead. Cook meat alone in broth for 20 minutes. Add potatoes *after* celery and onion, and cook only 20 minutes.

Curried Fish
(Matjeri masala)

Since Suriname is on the coast and has many waterways, it is no surprise that seafood forms a major part of the diet.

The garam masala called for is a reddish or green north Indian curry powder, available in most markets. Yellow curry powder can be substituted.

4 good-size firm white fish filets
½ cup flour or breadcrumbs
3 T. vegetable oil
1 onion, diced
1 tsp. garlic, chopped
1 T. garam masala

1 tomato, chopped
1 cup fish stock
¼ tsp. dried chili flakes
  (optional)
salt and pepper to taste

Salt and pepper fish. Place fish and flour or breadcrumbs into a zip-top plastic bag, and shake to coat well. Remove fish, shake off any excess breading, and fry in oil until golden brown on both sides. Remove fish from pan, and set aside.

If fish has absorbed most of the oil, add more to make about 2 T. in pan. Fry onion until it just begins to brown, then add garlic and masala and stir for a minute or so. Add tomato and stir well.

Add stock (or bottled clam juice), chili flakes, and stir to mix. Return fish to pan, and simmer gently for 8 to 10 minutes. Serve with rice.

Creole Rice with Codfish

This also came from West Africa. You can use shrimp in place of the cod, but add them with the coconut milk toward the end of the cooking.

4 T. vegetable oil	½ lb. codfish
1 onion, sliced	1 cup rice
1 tsp. garlic, chopped	2 cups fish stock
2 tomatoes, diced	1 cup coconut milk
1 T. soy sauce	salt and pepper to taste

Heat oil in pot and fry onion pieces until they begin to brown. Add garlic, tomatoes, and soy sauce. Add codfish cut into bite-size pieces, and cook for a minute or two. Then stir in rice and stock (bottled clam juice works). Cover and simmer until rice is done (20 to 25 minutes). Stir in coconut milk and simmer a few minutes more. Season to taste with salt and pepper.

Indonesian Rice and Chicken (Nasi Goreng)

This is another very popular dish in Suriname, and as with all popular dishes, it has numerous variations. Just be sure to allow enough time for the rice to cool before preparing the other ingredients.

1 cup rice	salt and pepper to taste
2 cups chicken broth	1 tsp. garlic, chopped
2 boneless, skinless chicken breasts	½ tsp. dried shrimp powder
	½ tsp. fresh ginger, chopped
2 or 3 T. butter or oil	3 T. soy sauce
1 onion, diced	1 stalk celery, sliced thin

Cook rice in chicken broth until tender (20 minutes). Fluff with fork, and turn out on plate or cookie sheet to cool. Break up any clumps. This will help it brown properly later.

In a large frying pan cook chicken breasts in 1 T. butter or oil until done through and lightly browned on both sides (about 12 minutes). After removing it from the pan, let the chicken cool a little, then cut it into thin slices.

Add another T. butter or oil to pan in which chicken was cooked, and cook onion and garlic until onion begins to brown. Add shrimp powder (available in oriental markets) and ginger, and cook for a minute more.

Add rice and cook until rice begins to brown. Add more butter or oil if needed. Add soy sauce and celery slices and cook for a minute or two more (celery should still be a little crunchy). Add chicken slices and heat thoroughly. Season to taste.

Yam Stuffed Chicken

The original of this dish comes from West Africa. This modern adaptation illustrates some of the characteristic flavors of that important strand in Surinamese cuisine.

2 yams or sweet potatoes	½ tsp. marjoram
4 boneless, skinless chicken breasts	salt and pepper to taste
	½ cup flour
2 T. butter	oil for frying
1 onion, diced	

Peel and dice yams, and boil in water until tender (20 to 30 minutes) while you prepare the other ingredients. (Or use canned yams.)

Pound chicken breasts until they are flattened and have a fairly even thickness all over. You can use a meat mallet, a heavy frying pan, a heavy food can, etc., for this.

Melt butter, and fry onion in it until onion is softened but not browned. Add marjoram, and fry a minute more.

Drain yams when done, and mash thoroughly until they are mostly smooth. Add onion, and stir to mix well. Season with salt and pepper to taste.

Put ¼ of the yam mixture on each chicken piece, and tuck in ends and roll chicken to completely enclose the yams (like a chicken cordon bleu or chicken Kiev roll). Tie with string or use toothpicks to secure roll.

Season rolls with salt and pepper, and place in zip-top plastic bag with flour to coat thoroughly.

Remove chicken, shake off excess, and fry in medium hot oil until well browned on all sides. Remove pan from heat, cover, and let chicken steam a little from residual heat to make sure it is done through.

Serve with spicy peanut sauce (page 108) or a favorite gravy.

Beef and Broccoli

This Chinese dish may stand as representative of that important element of Surinamese cuisine.

1 lb. beef round steak, or similar
1 T. cornstarch
1 T. soy sauce
1 T. oyster or hoisin sauce
1 T. rice wine vinegar
2 T. vegetable oil
1 (10 oz.) pkg. frozen broccoli
½ cup or a little more beef broth
sesame oil (optional)
spring onion or sesame seeds

Cut beef into very thin (less than ¼ inch) slices. Putting it in the freezer for a half hour first makes it easier to slice. Mix cornstarch, soy sauce, oyster or hoisin sauce, and vinegar. (You can get these in the oriental section of your supermarket.) Put meat in to marinate for a half hour.

Remove beef from marinade, shake off excess liquid, pat dry, and cook in very hot oil for 3 minutes or so, stirring constantly. Use a wok for this if you have one. Remove beef and set aside.

In remaining oil, fry thawed broccoli (cut into bite-size pieces) for about 2 minutes. Add ¼ cup beef broth, reduce heat a little, and let braise a few minutes until broth has evaporated.

Add remaining broth and marinade, or make fresh marinade if you are concerned about contamination. Increase heat again and return beef to pan. Add a couple of drops of sesame oil (the cooking kind, not the health store version) if you like. You can also add a little more broth to make a thinner sauce.

Serve over rice. You can garnish this with rounds of spring onion or some sesame seeds.

Note: You can use 2 cups fresh broccoli florets in place of the frozen. These will need to braise a little longer, so you may need to add a little water if the broth evaporates before the broccoli is tender. You can also substitute a bell pepper for the broccoli and then you have pepper steak.

Lamb and Orange Stew

This dish brings together elements from several of Suriname's cultures, which make up its wonderfully varied society.

1½ lbs. lamb, cut in cubes
3 T. vegetable oil or butter
1 onion, diced
1 bell pepper, diced
salt and pepper to taste

1 tsp. cumin
1 tsp. marjoram
1 T. flour
2 cups beef broth
1 orange or ½ cup juice

Heat oil (or butter), and brown lamb. Add onion and pepper, and cook until they begin to brown. Add seasonings, and stir for a minute.

Add flour and stir well. Add broth and stir.

Zest orange and set zest aside. Peel and separate orange sections, and add to stew. Or pour in orange juice if you are using that instead of a whole orange.

Simmer for 40 to 45 minutes. Check for seasoning, and serve over rice. Garnish with orange zest.

Variations: Add 1½ cups canned garbanzo beans (also called chick peas or ceci) during last 15 minutes of cooking. You can also use beef, pork, or chicken in place of the lamb.

Chinese Salad

As the name says, this is another example of the Chinese cuisine, which has made such a contribution to the local recipes. It is surprisingly light and refreshing, and makes a good accompaniment to many other dishes.

1 carrot
2-inch section daikon radish
2 T. sugar
2 T. rice wine (or white) vinegar

1 cup water
pinch of salt
¼ tsp. celery seeds or sesame seeds

Peel carrot and daikon, and slice into very thin matchsticks. (You can, of course, use 2 carrots if daikon isn't readily available.)

Mix sugar, vinegar, water, and salt, and heat to near boiling. Let cool for 10 minutes, then add carrot and daikon. Stir.

Place in refrigerator to cool for an hour or so. Stir in celery or sesame seeds.

Divide carrots and daikon into 4 small bowls, and pour a bit of the liquid into each.

Note: Jicama makes a nice and more easily handled substitute for the daikon. A stalk of celery also works.

Curried Potatoes
(Alu Tarkari)

This is another contribution of Indian cuisine to the Surinamese table. It is good with chicken or fish especially.

Again, yellow curry powder can be substituted for the garam masala.

4 medium potatoes	2 tsp. garam masala or
2 T. vegetable oil	yellow curry powder
1 onion, diced	1½ cups water
1 tsp. garlic, chopped	½ tsp. sugar
	salt and pepper to taste

Peel the potatoes and cut each into 4 to 6 pieces.

Heat oil in skillet, and fry onion until the pieces just start to brown. Add garlic and stir for a minute more. Add garam masala or yellow curry powder and stir. Add potatoes and stir until they are coated with color from the curry.

Add water, sugar, salt and pepper, and boil on low heat for 20 minutes or until potatoes are tender and sauce is slightly thickened.

Note: If you use a cut-up chicken instead of the potatoes, you will have chicken curry (murgi tarkari) instead. This version may need a little more water and 20 minutes more (or so) to cook. You can also use bite-size pieces of boneless chicken breast, which should cook in the same amount of time as the potatoes.

Indonesian Rice Cakes
(Lontong)

These are generally used as a side dish with meat. The uniqueness here is not in seasoning (there really isn't any), but in the cooking method and resulting texture. Short-grained rice, which is stickier than long grain, works better here.

>1 cup rice
>3 cups water
>½ tsp. salt

Put rice and water in a heavy pot. Let rice soak for about an hour. Then bring to a boil and add salt.

Reduce heat, cover, and simmer about 30 minutes until most of the water is absorbed. Rice should be sticky. Remove from heat and let rice sit covered for 10 minutes.

Drain any remaining water, and turn rice out onto a platter to cool for about 15 minutes, or until you can handle it comfortably.

A standard recipe says to divide rice into 4 portions, roll into cylinders, seal each tightly in a piece of aluminum foil, and boil for about 2 hours more. Unfortunately, I found it nearly impossible to seal the packets really tightly, and a soggy mess was the result.

As with Czech knedliky, a microwave makes things much better. Divide rice into 4 portions, and roll each into a "log" inside a piece of wax paper sprayed on the inside with cooking spray to prevent sticking. Cook on high in microwave for 4 minutes, let cool a little, unwrap, and cut rice into 1-inch slices.

Braised Bok Choy

This Chinese cabbage has become quite popular worldwide. It has a delicate but slightly bitter (not unpleasant) taste. Serve with meat, poultry, or fish.

4 to 6 heads baby bok choy	1 T. butter
¾ cup chicken broth	salt and pepper to taste

Cut bok choy in half longwise. Bring broth to slow boil, and add butter, salt and pepper, and bok choy. Reduce heat and simmer, covered, for 7 or 8 minutes. Bok choy should be mostly tender but just a little crunchy. Season with a little soy sauce if you like.

Stewed Pumpkin

Put 2 to 3 cups pumpkin, peeled, seeded, and cut into chunks, in pot with 1 cup water and a bit of salt. Bring to boil, then reduce heat to simmer.

If you want an Indian flavor, add ½ tsp. of ground cardamom and the same of ground coriander. An alternative is to use 1 tsp. of the dry West Indian seasoning (page 96) given in the Caribbean Islands section. Cook until pumpkin is tender (20 to 30 minutes).

If a fresh pumpkin is too large or unavailable, you can substitute a butternut or acorn squash. Since these are very hard to peel raw, cut them in half and bake them for a half hour first. Orange sweet potatoes are another possibility.

Finally, you can use canned cooked pumpkin (not pumpkin pie mix), omit water, and heat gently with seasonings. This is mashed pumpkin, so you won't have the texture of the chunks, but it *is* pumpkin, and you can get it all year, not just at Halloween.

Tangy Fruit Cream

This drink is neither sweet nor sour, but is surprisingly refreshing.

For each serving combine:

> 1 heaping T. plain active culture yogurt
> 1 T. sugar
> ¾ cup milk
> ¼ cup orange juice
> ¼ cup coconut milk
> a dash of cinnamon (optional)

Note: You can also use mango, guava, or papaya juice or nectar instead of the orange.

Rice Pudding

This recipe will make four very large or six smaller servings.

1 cup rice	½ cup sugar
2 cups water	1 tsp. cinnamon
1 cup evaporated milk	¼ tsp. salt
½ cup whole milk	¾ cup fruit

Bring rice and water to a boil, reduce heat, cover, and simmer for 12 to 15 minutes. Rice will be mostly but not completely cooked. Drain.

While rice is cooking, in another pot heat evaporated milk, whole milk, sugar, cinnamon, and salt. Add partially cooked rice, and simmer another 10 minutes or so until rice is tender. Remove from heat, and allow to cool for 10 to 12 minutes.

Stir in bite-size pieces of fruit. Bananas are good, as are mango and papaya (canned works fine). Peaches are less authentic, but are good too. Mix and match as you like.

Central America

Nicaragua, Honduras, Costa Rica

Moravians have been active in Nicaragua since 1849, mostly among the Miskitu and Creole peoples of the east coast. Work spread to Honduras in 1930, and Moravian presence in Costa Rica was established in the last decades of the 20th century.

As noted above, the continental provinces of North America have recently been enriched by the immigration of Moravians from Central America, so this blended cuisine with its Caribbean, African, and Spanish elements is no longer "over there," but thankfully is "right here."

Black Bean Soup
(Sopa Negra)

This soup is popular all over the Caribbean and Central America, and versions vary not only from region to region, but household to household. The following is a general way of doing it, which you can vary according to your own taste.

3 T. vegetable oil	2 15-oz. cans black beans
1 carrot, diced	2 cups chicken broth
1 onion, diced	½ tsp. dried oregano
1 bell pepper, diced	½ tsp. ground cumin
1 T. chopped garlic	salt and pepper to taste

Garnishes: crumbled cooked bacon, grated onion, chopped cilantro, grated cheese, sour cream.

In a Dutch oven or large pot, heat oil and fry carrot for 3 or 4 minutes, then add onion and bell pepper, and cook until they soften. Add garlic, and fry for another minute.

Stir in beans (drained) and broth, and heat. Add oregano and cumin, reduce heat, and simmer for 15 minutes or longer. Taste, and add salt and pepper accordingly.

To make soup nice and thick, use a potato masher to crush some of the beans. An immersion blender works too. Garnish as desired.

Cassava Flatbread
(Bammie)

This apparently originated from the indigenous Arawaks on the island of Jamaica, but it is made in Central America too. It is of particular interest since it comes from pre-Columbian times. You can find cassava flour in some Hispanic markets, probably labeled as "yucca" flour.

> 2 cups cassava flour
> 1½ tsp. salt
> 1½ cups water (approx.)

Mix ingredients, and knead into a firm dough. Start with 1 cup of water and go up from there a little at a time as needed. Cover and let rest for a half hour.

Divide dough into quarters, and roll out into rounds (about 6 inches, more or less).

Cook in frying pan with a little oil until browned on both sides.

Note: These flatbreads will be dense and heavy, which is probably authentic. After trying the original, you might want to add ½ tsp. baking powder to the dough to lighten it a little.

Honduran Thick Tortillas
(Pupusas)

These are very characteristic, easy to make, and can be filled with all sorts of good things. The ingredients for the dough are simplicity itself, though you may need to make it several times until you get a feel for just the right consistency. Also be sure to seal the filling inside very well so it doesn't leak, but even if it does, it's not usually disastrous.

> 2 cups masa harina (cornmeal flour)
> ½ tsp. salt
> 1 to 1½ cups warm water (approx.)

Mix masa harina (available in most markets) and salt with enough water to make a moist but fairly firm dough. If you use "instant" masa harina, it will require more water than "regular." Add water a little at a time until it feels right. Knead well. Cover and let rest for about 10 minutes.

Divide dough into 8 balls. It may be a good idea to try pressing one thin at this point. If it falls apart or has large splits at the edge, mix all the dough back together, and add a little more water. If it is too sticky, put dough back together, and add a little more masa. Unlike biscuits or pie crusts, this dough isn't harmed by remixing.

Pupusas can be made unfilled, and you may want to try them that way first. For filled and yummy pupusas, take each ball and make a deep indentation in it, pressing out until you get a hollow sphere. Place a spoonful of filling (see below) into the cavity, work sides up to cover, and press to seal completely.

Place a sealed ball between two sheets of plastic wrap or a plastic storage bag with the top cut off and the sides opened. The thicker plastic of the bag works better.

If you have a tortilla press, use that to press the ball inside the plastic into a circle about ¼ inch thick. If you don't have a press, place ball in plastic on a flat firm surface, and use a heavy flat-bottomed frying pan to press evenly. Repeat with each ball.

Cook each pupusa in a hot heavy pan (cast iron works best) for a minute or two on each side until dough is firm and brown spots appear. Cover to keep warm until all are cooked. It is best to prepare pupusas close to serving time. They tend to become leathery if kept too long.

Fillings:

Popular fillings include grated white cheese, chicharrones (crumbled fried pork rinds from a Hispanic market), or bacon in a little tomato sauce and refried beans. You can also use a combination of these. You will need a little less than a cup total of filling for the 8 pupusas.

Nicaraguan Hot Meat Pies
(Empanadas)

These also come in countless variations. The following is derived from Annette T. Robinson, who was born in Bluefields, Nicaragua, but now lives in Winston-Salem. Our thanks go out to her.

½ medium onion, chopped
½ medium bell pepper, chopped
1 tsp. salt
½ tsp. ground annatto (achiote)
5 or 6 slices stale bread
½ hot pepper, seeded
¼ tsp. garlic powder
1 lb. hamburger
⅓ cup vegetable oil
dough for 2 pie crusts, homemade or bought

In a food processor combine all ingredients except meat, oil, and dough. (Annatto or achiote is a yellow coloring agent available in Hispanic markets. If you don't have annatto, use a little food coloring or tumeric.) Add ⅓ to ½ cup water, and grind well.

Pour mixture into a large skillet with the meat and oil. Mix well, and cook on medium heat, breaking up pieces and stirring continuously until well done.

Make your favorite pie dough for a two-crust pie or use refrigerated rolled crusts. **Note:** Preformed frozen crust in pans will not work. If you are starting from scratch, Sr. Robinson says you can add ½ tsp. Bijol® powder to the dough to give it an orange color. (This is a brand-name product consisting of annato, fillers, and coloring. Check your Hispanic market for this.)

Roll out dough to a little less than ¼ inch thickness, and cut it in circles "about the size of a small saucer."

Fill with 1 T. meat mixture. Fold over, and press edges together. Place on a cookie sheet. Take a fork and make small holes on top. Bake in a preheated 375° oven for 20 to 30 minutes.

Note: You can cut down on the hot pepper if you need to. As a variation, you can also add some cumin or oregano along with the garlic for a little different seasoning. Also unless you are feeding a very large group, a half recipe will probably be enough.

Central American Tamales (Nacatamales)

These are a little different from what you have had in a Mexican restaurant. We thank Sam Gray and his extended family, who have long connection with Moravian work in Nicaragua and Honduras, for their personal recipe for these. In keeping with the openness and generosity of the people in this region, the original recipe would feed a small village. I have cut it down to make about eight tamales. You can double or triple it as needed.

½ lb. pork in small cubes
good dash of garlic and
    onion powder
salt to taste
pinch each ground annato and
    Bijol® powder
⅓ cup large canned green peas
½ large onion
¼ bell pepper

1 potato, peeled
vegetable oil
hot pepper (habañero)
½ cup rice
½ cup instant corn
    masa (approx.)
banana leaves, aluminum
    foil, and string for wrapping

Heat 2 tsp. oil in frying pan, and cook meat with garlic and onion powder, salt, annatto, and Bijol®. (These are yellow coloring agents available in Hispanic markets. If you can't find these, use a couple drops of food coloring or a good dash of ground tumeric.) When meat is almost done add 2 T. or so of water, cover, and cut off heat.

Slice onion, bell pepper, and potato. Wash rice and set aside.

Wash banana leaves well in sink. Rinse three or four times. You may find banana leaves in a Hispanic or Filipino market. If not, some recipes call for corn husks. You can find those dried in Hispanic markets, but they will need to soak a few hours in warm water to soften. If all else fails, use just the aluminum foil.

In a deep dish or pot mix ½ cup of the masa with ½ cup warm water from the faucet. Keep adding water until the masa is very soft. (If you go too far and make a liquid, add a little more masa.) Add ¼ cup medium hot oil to masa, and stir well. Add a dash of Bijol® powder and a little salt.

Cut foil about 14 inches long and lay on flat surface. Place a piece of banana leaf or corn husk on top. Put 1 heaping T. of masa in center and spread a little. Make two holes in masa and fill with 1 tsp. rice and 1 tsp. peas. Add some sliced onion and strips of bell pepper and a slice or two of potato. Add a few cubes or so of meat and some hot pepper which you have mashed in a little of the juice from the meat along with some vegetable oil.

Fold bottom of leaf up over filling, then fold in the sides, and then fold the top down over all. Fold foil over leaf packet to make a secure package and tie with string.

Fill a Dutch oven or other large pot about two-thirds full of water, and bring to a boil. Put nacatamales into slowly boiling water and cook for at least 4 hours. Remove from water, open packages, and they are ready to eat.

Note from the Grays: Can be frozen and good up to three months. Just remove from freezer, place in hot water, and boil for 1 hour.

Note: Do not eat the banana leaf or corn husk.

Corn Tamales
(Tamales de Elote)

These tamales are meatless but very flavorful and typical.

Take 8 banana leaf pieces as for nacatamales above. Some versions instead use dried corn husks that have been soaked in water several hours to soften. Again, the foil alone can do if necessary.

1½ cups corn kernels, fresh, frozen, or canned	¾ to 1 cup water (approx.)
1½ cups masa harina	3 T. solid vegetable shortening
1 tsp. salt	3 T. butter
	1½ tsp. baking powder

If using fresh corn, cut kernels off cob with sharp knife. If using frozen, thaw. If using canned, drain. Purée in a food processor for a few seconds. The corn should still have a good number of chunks in it.

Mix the masa harina (Mexican corn flour) with the salt and a little water at a time to make a medium soft dough. Add corn and mix thoroughly.

Using a hand-held mixer, whip the shortening (the original recipe calls for lard), butter, and baking powder until the mixture becomes light.

Combine corn mixture and shortening mixture. Mix until blended thoroughly.

Take a piece of banana leaf or softened corn husk, shake off excess water, and put about ¼ cup of corn-dough in the center. Fold, wrap in foil, and tie securely as with nacatamales above.

Boil the tamales for half an hour. Check one to make sure the inside is fairly firm. If not, cook up to 15 minutes more. Discard banana leaf or corn husk and serve tamales with meats, stews, or prepared chili sauce.

Rondon (Rundown)

Thanks again to the extended Gray family for this fish stew recipe. The original makes 10 servings, but I have cut it here to a generous 4. You can easily double it again for a larger group.

1 good-size cassava (yucca)	1 15-oz. can coconut milk
1 green plantain	1 6-oz. can tomato paste
salt and pepper to taste	1½ lbs. shrimp
½ onion, diced	1 lb. fresh fish filets
1 clove (1 T.) garlic, chopped	

Boil small pieces of peeled cassava and plantain in water to cover. When cassava and plantain are soft, add salt and pepper, onion, and garlic.

Shake coconut milk well and add to cassava, plantain, and water. Stir in tomato paste.

Bring ingredients to a boil, and then reduce heat to medium before adding shrimp and fish. Cook slowly until fish is firm. Remove from heat and serve with rice.

Chicken with Rice
(Arroz con Pollo)

This dish is prevalent in countless variations throughout Central America and the Caribbean. This is an adaptation of a Costa Rican version supplied by Barbara Giesler, who served with her husband, John, for many years in Nicaragua.

5 T. butter
2 onions, sliced or diced
1 tsp. garlic
1 chicken, cut into pieces
4 tomatoes (fresh or canned)
½ cup sliced celery
2 bell peppers (red, green, or both)
½ tsp. *each* oregano and thyme

¼ tsp. marjoram
1 cup rice
2 cups chicken broth
1 small (5 oz.) bottle stuffed olives
½ cup raisins (optional)
1 cup frozen green peas, cooked

Fry 1 onion in 2 T. butter until soft but not brown. Add garlic, stir, and add chicken. Cook until chicken just begins to brown. Add tomatoes, celery, peppers (cut in strips), and herbs. Lower heat, cover, and steam until chicken is done (about 30 minutes). If it starts to burn, add just a little water.

As chicken cooks, in another pan fry the other onion in 3 T. butter until soft but not browned. Some recipes call for adding saffron here to enhance color. Saffron is very expensive, so you may want to use a little annatto or yellow food coloring or 1 tsp. turmeric instead, or omit this altogether. Add rice and stir for about 5 minutes until rice just starts to brown. Add broth, reduce heat, cover, and simmer for 20 minutes until rice is soft. Remove cover and let sit on burner for a minute to dry out excess moisture. Stir if necessary to keep from scorching.

If desired, you can remove chicken from bone, then return it to the pan with tomatoes, etc. Add drained olives, raisins, and peas. Add salt and pepper to taste. Let simmer for a few minutes, and stir chicken and tomato mixture with rice. Check for seasoning and serve.

Variation: Use four boneless, skinless chicken breasts instead of the whole chicken. This will need less simmering to get done.

Vigoron

This is from a recipe graciously supplied by Sr. Annette T. Robinson. Vigoron is very popular as a snack or as part of a larger meal.

2 lbs. cassava (yucca)
1 lb. cabbage
1 cup vinegar
½ tsp. salt

2 large dill pickles
1 T. prepared mustard
pork rinds
pepper (habañero)

Peel cassava and cook in about 2 to 3 cups of water with salt until soft. Sr. Robinson says to cook the cassava "not too well done." Cut into small pieces. (In a pinch potatoes could substitute for the cassava.)

Shred cabbage and place in deep dish. Add vinegar, salt, pickles cut into small pieces, and mustard. Mix together. You can add some of the seeded pepper to taste.

Serve cassava and some fried pork rinds ("chicharrones" from a Hispanic market) with cabbage mixture and some of its sauce on top.

Miskitu Tortilla

Thanks to Sam Gray for this treat. Compare it to Mitzi Kimball's "roti" (page 100) in the Caribbean section.

1 lb. flour (approx. 3 cups)
1 tsp. salt
1½ tsp. baking powder
1 T. solid shortening

Mix the flour, salt, baking powder, and shortening together in a mixing bowl.

Form the dough into a ball by adding small amounts of cool water until the dough is slightly rubbery.

Spread the dough out on a flat surface such as a bread board, knead 20 to 30 strokes, and roll until flat and about ½ inch thick.

Cut into triangles or rectangles, **or** roll bits of the dough into balls and flatten out into circular shapes.

Score the shapes with a knife to allow the dough to breathe (and soak up the oil!).

Heat oil (about ¼ to ½ inch deep) in a frying pan.

Fry the tortillas until golden brown on both sides.

Serve with choice of topping (butter, honey, jam), or eat with eggs and refried beans.

Rice and Beans (Three Ways)
Gallo Pinto

Rice cooked with beans (or beans cooked with rice) is a staple in all of Central America as well as the Caribbean Islands, East Africa, and elsewhere. Do not be surprised to get them for breakfast as well as lunch and dinner in those areas. As with any favorite, there are countless variations in how to prepare this dish. Sam Gray provides the following three versions from Moravians in Central America:

Compare these with the Tanzanian beans and rice recipe (page 196).

A. Gallo Pinto (Rice and Beans)

(Costa Rica version)

1½ to 2 cups cooked black beans	2 cups white rice
8 to 10 sprigs cilantro, divided	3 cups chicken broth or water
1 small or medium onion, divided	½ tsp. salt
½ small red or yellow sweet pepper, divided (optional)	1 T. vegetable oil
	1 to 3 T. oil for frying

If beans are dried, cover with water and soak overnight. If they are fresh, just rinse them off. Drain the beans and add fresh water to an inch above the top of the beans, salt, and bring to a boil. Cover the pan and reduce heat to very low simmer until beans are soft (about 3 hours).

Note: Sam assures me that for this and the two following recipes you can use a 15- or 16-oz. can of beans along with some of their liquid in place of the dried or fresh ones with their long soaking and cooking times.

Chop cilantro, onion, and sweet pepper very fine.

Add 1 T. oil to a large pan and sauté the dry rice for 2 minutes over medium high heat, then add half of the cilantro, chopped onion, and sweet pepper, and sauté another 2 minutes. Add water or chicken broth, bring to a boil, cover, and reduce heat to simmer until rice is tender (20 to 25 minutes).

Keep a significant amount of the "black water" (½ to 1 cup) with the beans. This is what gives the rice its color and some of its flavor. Increase heat, and cook the rice, beans and "black water," the rest of the cilantro, chopped onion, and sweet pepper together in vegetable oil for a few minutes. Sprinkle with a little fresh chopped cilantro just before serving.

B. Gallo Pinto (Rice and Beans)

(Nicaragua version)

2 T. vegetable oil
2 large onions, sliced thin
2 cups cooked red beans

¼ cup water (or liquid left over from cooking the beans!)
1 cup cooked white rice

Beans: If you choose to cook your own beans, place 1 cup of dry red beans, 1 or 2 mashed garlic cloves, and enough water to cover in a pressure cooker and cook for 15 to 20 minutes. Do not add salt, as it will toughen the beans. Canned beans to which you add 1 T. chopped garlic can be used instead. Drain them, but save ¼ cup of the liquid.

Rice: Converted rice works best. It can be made in the rice cooker if you prefer, but watch the water/rice ratio and cooking time; the rice needs to be firm, not sticky.

Heat the oil in a heavy pot and sauté onion until lightly golden. Add the cooked beans and liquid. Stir gently and continuously over low heat for about 5 minutes; the beans should remain whole, not mashed.

Add the cooked rice and continue to stir for about 10 minutes. Taste and add a little salt if desired.

C. Gallo Pinto (Rice and Beans)

(Miskitu style)

2 T. vegetable oil	½ to 1 cup coconut milk
2 large onions, sliced thin	1 cup white rice
2 cups cooked red beans	2 cups water (approx.)

Beans: If you choose to cook your own beans, place 1 cup of dry red beans, 1 or 2 mashed garlic cloves, and enough water to cover in a pressure cooker and cook for 15 to 20 minutes. Do not add salt, as it will toughen the beans. Canned beans to which you add 1 T. chopped garlic can be used instead. Drain, but save ¼ cup liquid.

Rice: Heat 2 T. of oil in a heavy pot and sauté the onions until lightly golden. Wash the rice; drain, but leave it slightly wet. Add the rice to the hot oil and onions. Stir gently for about a minute. Then add the coconut milk with enough water to cover rice by at least ½ inch.

When the rice has soaked up at least half of its liquid, add the cooked beans with their liquid. Cook until the rice is tender and the liquid has been soaked up.

Grilled Steak
(Carne Asada)

This is not terribly different from everybody's steak cooked on a charcoal or gas grill, but the marinade gives it a Central American flair.

1 large (1½ lbs. or so) flank
    or skirt steak
4 T. vegetable oil
1 onion, sliced thin

⅔ cup orange juice
¼ tsp. ground cumin
2 tsp. garlic, minced
salt and pepper to taste

Marinate the steak for an hour or several with the other ingredients in a zip-top plastic bag. Go light on or omit the salt at this point. Too much salt in the marinade will dry out the meat.

Pat the meat dry, and cook on a hot grill on both sides until outside is nicely browned and inside is as rare or done as you like it, usually 7 minutes a side for medium. Now add salt as desired.

Let the meat rest for 15 minutes for juices inside to redistribute and not all run out at the first slice.

Slice meat into thin strips across the grain, and use to make tacos, burritos, etc. Combine with grilled onions and bell peppers in soft tortillas, and you have fajitas. Or serve sliced like London broil with a prepared green or red chili sauce with rice and vegetables. Feel free to add other spices (oregano, rosemary, red chilies, etc.) to the marinade or as you are grilling, as you like.

Baked Nicaraguan Ripe Plantain

We again thank Sr. Annette T. Robinson for this recipe.

4 very ripe and soft plantains
4 tsp. cinnamon
1 cup sugar
1½ cups grated mozzarella
   or Parmesan cheese
1 stick butter
1 cup milk

Peel the plantains, cut each into several pieces, and fry the pieces in hot oil until they begin to brown.

Place a layer of plantain into a small greased baking dish. Sprinkle with cinnamon, sugar, and cheese. Put on another layer of plantain, add more cinnamon, sugar, and cheese, and repeat until plantains are used up, ending with a layer of cheese.

Pour milk over all, and put butter, cut in small pieces, over the top.

Cover with foil, and bake in a 350° oven for 25 to 30 minutes until top is golden brown and cheese is melted.

Note: If you omit the cheese, this makes a nice dessert also. Sam Gray says he likes to use green instead of ripe plantains. Those may need to cook a little longer.

Fried Plantains with Cream
(Plátanos Fritos con Crema)

This is a less fancy version of the above. Fry the plantain pieces in butter until they are brown and tender. Drain and salt to taste. Serve warm with a dollop of sour cream (and a little grated cheese if you like).

Potato Salad with Cheese Sauce
(Papas a la Huancína)

The original of this recipe comes from Peru, but has been adapted in Honduras and Nicaragua too.

4 potatoes
½ cup grated white cheese
½ cup milk
¼ hot pepper, chopped
2 T. vegetable oil

up to ¼ cup cracker or bread crumbs
¼ to ½ tsp. turmeric or ground annatto
salt and pepper to taste

Peel potatoes, cut into 4 to 6 pieces each, and boil in salted water until tender, about 20 minutes. Drain and cool.

Put cheese, milk, pepper, and oil in blender, and pulse until smooth. With processor running, add enough cracker or bread crumbs to thicken sauce to salad dressing consistency. Blend in turmeric or annatto for color, and salt and pepper to taste. If the sauce needs a brighter flavor, add a little lemon or lime juice.

Pour sauce over potatoes. You can serve this as a cold dish by itself or as part of a salad with lettuce, tomatoes, etc.

Fried Yucca (Cassava)

Sam Gray brought this to the Southern Province staff Christmas gathering in 2007, and it was unbelievably good, like really excellent French fries but better. I asked him if you just peel, cut, and fry the yucca. He was quick to say, "I learned the hard way you have to boil them first!" Thanks for the tip.

To prepare, peel yuccas (cassavas), and boil whole in water until firm but tender.

Let cool a bit, and cut into thick strips as for English "chips" (see page 50).

Put strips into deep hot oil, and stir occasionally until they are a nice golden brown.

Remove from oil, drain, salt liberally, and serve while hot.

Latin American Caramel Spread
(Dulce de Leche)

You can use this spread on bread or as a filling between layers of a cake, etc. You can even warm it again and pour it over cake, ice cream, or puddings. It's good enough to eat by itself as candy, but you probably should resist too much of that.

Use about 3 parts milk to 1 part sugar and stir to dissolve. Add a good pinch of baking soda (This keeps the end result soft.) Bring slowly up to a boil, then reduce heat immediately to a simmer. Stir frequently. It will take a little over an hour to become thick and a golden caramel brown. Remove from heat, stir in a little vanilla, and allow to cool some before using. (The final amount will be half to two-thirds of what you started with.)

I understand that a shortcut (from Mexico) is to use a can of sweetened condensed milk instead of the milk and sugar above. This will caramelize quicker, but the end product is just a little different. It's still delicious, though.

Nicaraguan "Coco" Cake
(Que quiste, Malanga, Yaticia, Yautia)

This and the following two recipes are from Annette T. Robinson again.

In this dish the "coco" has nothing to do with chocolate or coconut, but is another name for the vegetable known as "yaticia" or the more widely used "yautia." It may also be labeled "coco malanga." Sr. Robinson assures us that yaticia is available in Hispanic markets. Sam Gray says if you can't find yaticia in your area, sweet potato could make a substitute of sorts.

4 *red* cocos (yaticia, yautia, etc.)
1 medium-size cassava (yucca)
2 cups sugar (or more to taste)
2 tsp. cinnamon
1 tsp. nutmeg

2 tsp. vanilla
1 (14-oz.) can coconut milk
1 stick butter, softened
½ cup evaporated milk

Peel cocos and cassava. Wash and grate them into a large bowl, and add the rest of the ingredients except the evaporated milk. Stir well. If 2 cups of sugar do not make it sweet enough, add more. ("Needs to be sweet," says Sr. Robinson.)

Pour into a large deep baking pan or dish ("so it won't boil over"). Cook slowly in preheated oven at 200° for 1 to 1½ hours ("very important"), then add evaporated milk and bake at 350° until it is golden brown and forms a very nice custard.

Nicaraguan Coconut Tarts (Guizadas)

3 (8-oz.) packs frozen coconut, thawed
2 cups sugar
3 tsp. cinnamon
½ stick butter, softened
1 tsp. vanilla

Mix all ingredients and set aside.

Make or buy your favorite pie crust and roll out dough. Frozen pre-formed dough in pans doesn't work well. Cut with a large round cookie cutter. Pinch or squeeze edges together to form a cup. Place rounds on a cookie sheet and fill with 1 T. full of coconut mixture.

Bake in preheated oven at 400° for 20 to 25 minutes until slightly browned.

Note: The above recipe will make an awful lot of tarts (48 or so), so you may want to make only a fraction of it. On the other hand, they are so good you may need lots and lots for your friends and relations.

Also putting the pastry cups into the cups of a non-stick mini muffin pan instead of cooking them on a sheet will help them hold their shape.

Coconut Squares
(Dulce de Coco)

Crust:

½ cup butter, 1 cup flour, ½ cup sugar

Mash together, and put into a pan or dish. It should cover the bottom and can come a little way up the sides. Bake in preheated oven at 350° for 5 minutes or until lightly browned. Remove crust and increase oven to 375°.

Filling:

1 cup sugar
½ tsp. salt
2 cups coconut

2 eggs
3 T. flour
1 tsp. vanilla

If coconut is frozen, thaw it out. Mix filling ingredients together. Add to already baked crust and bake for 15 to 20 minutes. Cool, then cut in squares.

Cake of Three Milks
(Pastel de Tres Leches)

This dessert is surprisingly simple but delicious. I understand that both Honduras and Nicaragua lay passionate claim to it. No matter where it started, it is good.

Make your favorite yellow cake batter (there is no shame in a high quality boxed mix). Pour into a 9 x 13-inch baking pan or two 8- or 9-inch round pans, and bake according to your recipe's instructions.

When done, remove from oven and allow to cool. With a large fork make holes all over surface and down into cake.

Mix 1 cup each of whole milk, evaporated milk, and sweetened condensed milk. Pour slowly all over cake, allowing it to seep in. This seems like a lot of milk, but the cake will take it.

Cover and refrigerate for several hours to allow cake to absorb milks.

Cut and serve. Some recipes call for icing the cake with whipped cream, but it is plenty rich and flavorful without it. You could put some tropical fruit over each piece if you like, and that is delightful, but again it really doesn't need it.

Nicaraguan Bun

Barbara Giesler gives the source for this recipe, which the Nicaraguans speak of as singular, not plural:

"This is the recipe for buns which are very popular in Nicaragua. I wanted to know how to make them and asked for a recipe. I was told that no one had a recipe written down, so I invited a friend (Sr. Myrtle Harrison) to our house and asked her to make some for us. As we went along, I measured everything and recorded it."

Barbara also notes that the original recipe makes a very sweet bun, but they are very good with half the sugar. We will give the reduced sugar version, but if you want to be absolutely authentic and your arteries can stand it, double the 2 cups sugar called for here.

Note: This recipe makes a *lot* of buns. You may want to make a half recipe.

2 T. dry yeast	3 tsp. vanilla
1 cup warm water	1 tsp. ground cloves
1 tsp. sugar	1 tsp. nutmeg
1½ cups flour	½ tsp. allspice
3 cups milk	¾ cup shortening
1 T. salt	1 cup raisins
2 cups sugar	flour to make stiff dough,
2 tsp. cinnamon	about 9 to 10 cups

Mix yeast, water, 1 tsp. sugar, and 1½ cups flour. Let stand until foamy, then add and mix the rest of the ingredients.

Let rise 2 hours or until doubled in size, shape into pieces about the size of a tennis ball, let rise again for about an hour, and bake about 15 minutes in a preheated 325° oven. Rotate pans for even browning.

Glaze them with a mixture of 1 cup powdered sugar and 2 T. water while buns are still warm.

- Tabora
- Sikonge

TANZANIA

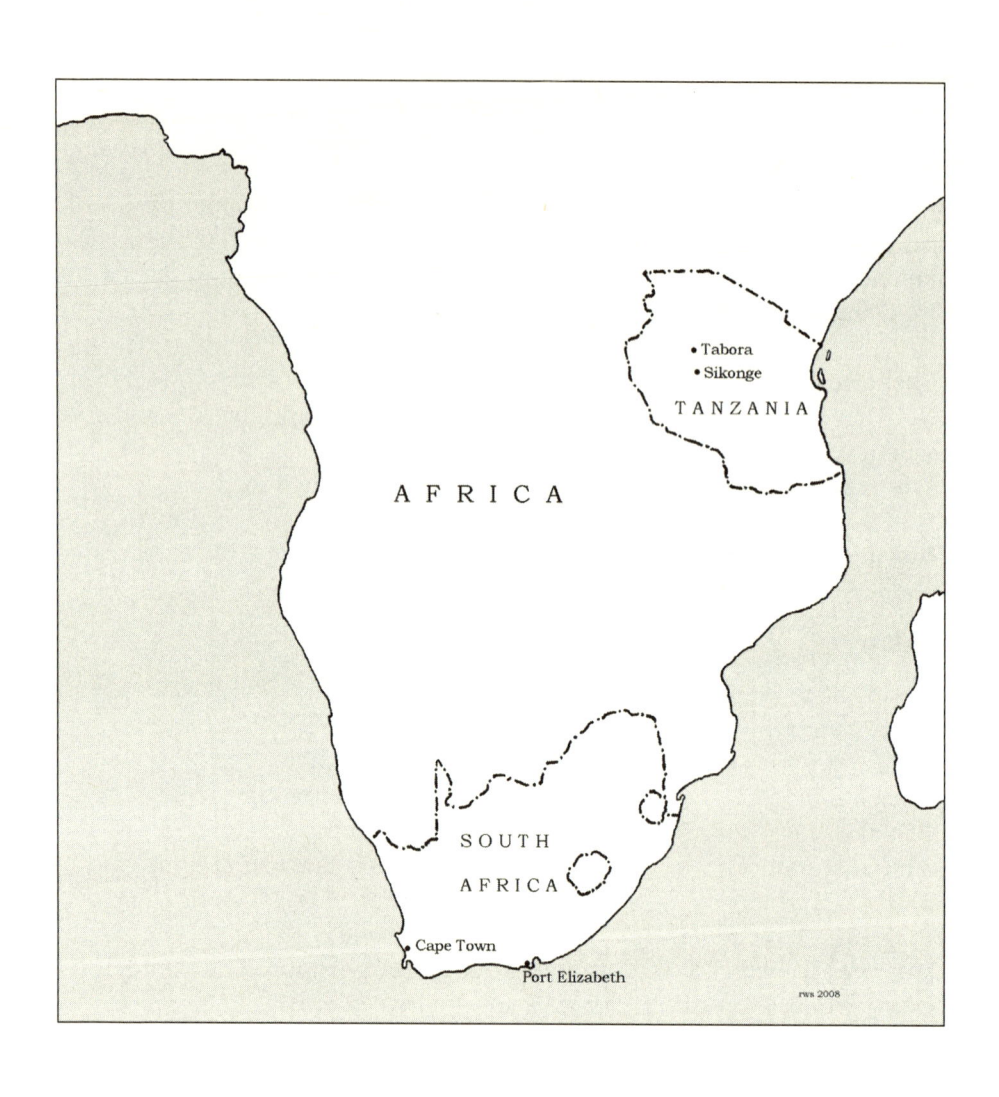

AFRICA

SOUTH AFRICA

Cape Town
Port Elizabeth

rws 2008

South Africa

Moravian work in South Africa began in 1737. After five years the first convert was baptized, but now that the work was having success, colonial officials forced the mission to close. When Moravian church workers were allowed to return in 1792 they found a great pear tree that Georg Schmidt, the first missionary, had planted. From there the Moravian presence spread. Work in the eastern part of South Africa began in 1828. Because of political racial regulations, there had to be two provinces in South Africa for many years, but today our Moravian Brothers and Sisters can be united administratively as they have always been united in their hearts and souls.

South Africa is a vast country, so obviously there are regional variations in the cuisine. Dishes often reflect the combination of various cultures that have come together there. In all areas, the dishes are plentiful and delicious.

I asked American members going to the 2007 Unity Brass Festival in South Africa to bring me back recipes from their hosts and other friends they met there. Bart Collins (of the Moravian Music Foundation) and Ray Gatland were glad to help, and I received about 150 recipes to use or adapt for our benefit. Here are a few of the best.

Fish Spread

1 large firm white fish filet or a 6 oz. can of crabmeat
¼ bell pepper, chopped very fine
¼ onion, grated or chopped fine

½ tsp. Worcestershire sauce
1 T. catsup
2 to 3 T. mayonnaise

If using fish filet, poach in water with a few slices of onion, a bay leaf, and salt and pepper to taste. When fish is firm, remove from water, cool, and flake.

If using canned crab, drain liquid and pick through crab to be sure there are no stray shell parts.

Mix all the other ingredients to make a dressing and gently fold in the fish or crab. Serve on bread or crackers.

Pineapple Salad

Pineapple is popular and quite plentiful in much of South Africa. This is a good example of its many uses.

Make 1 large or 4 individual tossed salads with lettuce, sliced onion, cucumber, celery, radishes, etc., as desired (but not tomatoes).

Dress salad with your favorite "ranch" dressing, or try the following. The little bit of extra trouble is worth it.

Mix together ¼ cup mayonnaise, 2 T. milk, 1 T. sugar, and 1 tsp. vinegar or lemon juice. If you like a lot of dressing, you can make a double batch.

Sprinkle about 1 cup pineapple chunks, fresh or canned, over dressed salad(s). Garnish with poppy seeds and slivered almonds or chopped peanuts as desired.

Chicken Salad Port Elizabeth

2 cups cooked white meat chicken, cubed or shredded
2 tsp. vegetable oil
¼ to ½ tsp. curry powder (optional)
½ medium onion, finely chopped
½ cup celery, thinly sliced
2 T. chicken broth
2 tsp. lemon juice
1 tsp. catsup
2 T. apricot jam
⅔ cup mayonnaise

Bring oil in pan to medium heat, add curry powder, and stir. Add onion and celery, and stir until just softened but not browned.

Mix chicken broth, lemon juice, catsup, and apricot jam, and stir until blended. Add to pan with onion and celery, and cook for a couple of minutes. Let cool to room temperature, and stir in mayonnaise.

Fold in chicken and refrigerate to blend flavors.

Serve with lettuce, tomatoes, pineapple, mandarin orange slices, etc., for a summer plate, or use to make sandwiches.

Meat Triangles

Bart Collins vouches for the "scrumptiousness" of small meat pastries very close to these.

¼ pound ground beef
¼ medium onion, finely chopped
¼ tsp. garlic powder
pinch each of ground allspice,
   curry powder, ground cumin,
   ground cloves, cinnamon
¼ tsp. marjoram

½ tsp. Worcestershire sauce
salt and pepper to taste
1 tsp. flour
2 T. milk

6 sheets phyllo pastry
4 T. butter, melted

Preheat oven to 350°.

Thaw one packet of phyllo pastry, available in frozen pastry section of your market. Take 6 sheets and cover with a slightly damp towel. (They dry out and get brittle very quickly.) Return rest of dough to package and refrigerate for future use.

Break up hamburger and fry until it just begins to brown. Add onion, stir, and cook for 2 or 3 minutes.

Add seasonings and mix well. Sprinkle lightly with flour, and add milk to bind together. Remove from heat and cool 10 minutes.

When meat is nearly cool, take a sheet of thawed phyllo pastry and brush with melted butter. Keep remaining sheets covered with a slightly dampened towel.

Put another sheet of phyllo on top of the first, brush with butter, and repeat with a third sheet.

Put long edge of stack toward you and use a pizza cutter or very sharp knife to divide it into 4 equal strips. If you want smaller pieces, cut phyllo into 6 strips and put less filling on each.

Put a heaping spoonful of meat mixture onto bottom corner of phyllo strip. Fold phyllo over the meat upward and over to make a triangle, fold resulting triangle straight up, then over again to make a triangle, and so on up the strip. Someone has described this as "like folding a United States flag." Repeat with all 4 strips, cover, and set aside.

Repeat procedure with the remaining phyllo sheets, butter, and meat mixture.

Place triangles with loose edge down on a baking sheet, and brush tops with butter. Bake in a preheated 350° oven for 7 to 10 minutes until nice and brown.

Let cool until they can be handled, and serve as finger food. If leftovers need to be reheated, place on cookie sheet in a preheated 250° oven for a few minutes.

Note: Instead of phyllo dough you could use thin rolled pastry dough circles, folded over the filling into a sealed half moon shape. Or if you still prefer triangles, cut dough into squares, put on filling, and fold diagonally.

Butternut Squash Soup

You may find some similarities in this dish to the fresh tomato soup (page 46) given in the Great Britain section. Both are a rich delight.

1 lb. butternut squash, peeled and diced	¼ tsp. nutmeg
	¼ tsp. ginger
1 large potato or sweet potato	4 cups chicken broth
1 carrot	1 cup heavy cream
1 onion	salt and pepper to taste
1 tsp. cinnamon	3 T. butter

Raw butternut squash is very hard to peel and cut. To make things easier, split it in half, remove seeds, and roast squash in a preheated 350° oven for 30 minutes, then scoop from shell and chop as needed.

Melt butter in Dutch oven. Add butternut and other vegetables, peeled and chopped. Add cinnamon, nutmeg, ginger, and salt and pepper. Fry over medium heat for a few minutes, then add 1 cup broth, reduce heat, cover, and simmer for a half hour or so until vegetables are tender. Add more broth if pot starts to go dry.

Remove mixture from heat and let cool for 15 minutes or so. Puree to smooth consistency in a blender. You will need to do this in 2 or 3 batches.

Return to pot, add remaining broth, and heat until hot. Turn off heat and stir in cream. If it is too thick, add a little more milk or broth. Check for seasonings, and serve.

Chicken and Cheese Soup

3 T. butter
1 onion, finely diced
1 carrot, finely diced
1 stalk celery, sliced thin
2 T. flour

4 cups chicken broth
1 cup grated cheddar cheese
1 cup heavy cream
¼ tsp. ground nutmeg
1 cup diced cooked chicken

Melt butter over medium heat in Dutch oven. Add vegetables and cook until they are a bit softened but not browned. Sprinkle on flour, stir, and cook for a minute or so.

Slowly stir in chicken broth. Cook over low heat for 20 to 30 minutes until vegetables are tender. Then stir in cheese a little at a time until smoothly melted.

Lower heat to simmer, and stir in cream. Add the nutmeg. At the end, add the chicken and stir until it is warmed through.

Check for seasoning, and add salt and pepper to taste. (Taste first since the cheese may be salty.) Serve in bowls, and garnish with parsley or a dollop of sour cream if you wish.

Frikkadelle
(Meatballs)

These can be eaten plain as an appetizer or snack, or baked with a sauce as a main dish.

Meatballs:

1 lb. ground beef, pork, or lamb
½ medium onion, grated
½ tsp. garlic powder
1 T. chopped coriander leaves
   (cilantro)
salt and pepper as desired
1 egg, beaten
½ cup breadcrumbs (approx.)

Sauce:

1 cup tomato sauce
½ cup catsup
4 T. lemon juice or vinegar
3 T. brown sugar
1 tsp. onion powder
½ tsp. garlic powder
1 T. soy sauce
¼ tsp. liquid smoke (optional)
water as needed

Combine meat and other meatball ingredients, stirring after each couple of ingredients are added, especially after egg. Add breadcrumbs last as needed to stiffen so you can handle the mixture. It should still be rather wet at this point.

Divide mixture into 12 and roll into balls. Place in a single layer in an ovenproof container and bake, uncovered, for 15 to 20 minutes in a preheated 350° oven.

If you are using sauce, mix all ingredients, and add enough water to make it just a little thinner than regular tomato sauce. After the meatballs have cooked for the first 15 to 20 minutes, pour sauce over meatballs, cover, and bake another half hour.

If you are not using sauce, cover meatballs after the first 15 to 20 minutes, and bake another 20 to 30 minutes. Check halfway through to make sure they are not burning. If pan is dry, add a little water.

Note: The meatball mixture (without the egg and breadcrumbs) can also be used as stuffing for meat triangles (page 158) instead of the recipe given there. Just be sure to cook the meat and seasonings first.

Baked Fish

A country with as much coastline as South Africa is bound to eat a lot of seafood. Grilled fish is popular there as here. One recipe I saw was very like the fish pudding (page 95) in the Caribbean section, so that can be counted as a South African dish as well. The following is a little more complex but still easy to prepare.

4 filets flounder, cod, etc.
salt and pepper to taste
½ onion, grated
2 T. lemon juice

6 oz. plain yogurt
¾ cup breadcrumbs
1 T. mixed thyme and basil
4 T. butter

Preheat oven to 350°.

In an ovenproof dish, place fish filets in single layer, and season with salt and pepper. Mix onion, lemon juice, and yogurt, and spread liberally over fish. Sprinkle with breadcrumbs and herbs. Melt butter and pour over top.

Bake uncovered for 20 minutes, or until fish is firm. Serve with salad and vegetables.

Variations: Use half breadcrumbs and half Parmesan cheese for topping. Another version favors Dijon mustard instead of the lemon juice with the onion and yogurt.

Fish in Coconut Milk

4 filets flounder, cod, etc.
2 T. butter
1 onion, sliced thin
1 tomato, chopped (optional)

¼ tsp. cumin
¼ tsp. turmeric
2 cups coconut milk
salt and pepper to taste

Melt butter in large pan over medium heat. Fry onion slowly until softened but not browned. Add tomato, cumin, and turmeric, reduce heat, and stir for a couple minutes more. Pour in coconut milk, and stir. Add salted and peppered fish in one layer. Spoon some of the sauce on top of the fish. Cover and simmer for 10 minutes. Uncover, increase heat a little, and cook for a few minutes more, 3 to 5 probably, until fish is firm.

Serve with rice or other starch, and a salad.

Note: Those who like spicier dishes can add a bit of ginger or chopped green chili along with the cumin and turmeric.

Baked Pork Chops

Bart Collins reported this was a personal favorite served by his hosts during the 2007 Unity Brass Festival.

4 regular pork chops
2 T. vegetable oil
sage

1 onion, thinly sliced
salt and pepper to taste

Sauce

1 cup catsup
½ tsp. onion powder
½ tsp. garlic powder
2 T. brown sugar

½ tsp. liquid smoke
1 T. Worcestershire sauce
½ cup water

Season chops with salt, pepper, and a pinch of sage. Heat oil in an ovenproof pan (cast iron is best), and fry chops until they brown lightly on both sides. Separate onion rings and scatter over chops.

Make sauce by combining ingredients given. You can also use the sauce from the frikkadelle recipe (page 162) minus the extra water. Another alternative is a cup of your favorite barbecue sauce, thinned with ¼ to ½ cup water.

Pour sauce over chops, and bake uncovered in a preheated 325° oven for up to an hour or until sauce is almost caramelized. If the bottom of the pan begins to burn, add a little more water to the bottom of the pan, not on top of the chops.

Serve with rice, potatoes, or "pap" (page 180). Bart says a cold pasta salad goes particularly well with this also. Add a side of vegetables, and you have a hearty meal.

Note: You can use thick-cut pork chops, but fry them a little longer at the beginning, cover pan with foil, and bake for 15 or 20 minutes. Then uncover, and proceed to cook for another hour or so as above.

Braii

In South Africa "braii" (pronounced brī) refers to the method of cooking rather than a specific dish. It means cooked over an open fire. Today, charcoal or gas grills are often used. The main point is for people to get together outdoors, grill good meat with plenteous accompaniments, and generally have a good time.

If this reminds you of an American backyard barbecue, that's exactly the sort of thing it is. It doesn't matter whether the meat is beef, pork, chicken, sausages, or antelope, or what particular seasoning you use, the object is food and fellowship and plenty of both.

For a bit of a difference from an ordinary barbecue, you can use some of the seasoning combinations given in the Caribbean or other sections of this book. The tomato sauce given for frikkadelle above (page 162) makes a great barbecue sauce for grilled meats and chicken.

If you have the opportunity, try cooking over an open fire, campfire style. If not, you can still enjoy the spirit of braii.

Potjiekos

The name refers to the big iron pot ("potjie") in which the meal is cooked, traditionally outdoors over wood coals or charcoal. With a tight lid, a potjie is the predecessor of the modern electric slow cooker.

Potjiekos originated from European settlers in South Africa who took a "potjie" in their wagons, cooked over a campfire, and after eating loaded the pot with whatever was left in it back into their wagons for the next day's travel. Then more vegetables (potatoes, beans, tomatoes, such as they had) were added to the remaining stew, along with the game they had shot that day (rabbit, warthog, bush pig, or whatever).

Potjiekos today is accepted as a favorite of all the cultures that make up South Africa. Good food is good, wherever it comes from. A gathering for potjiekos is the same in spirit as for a braii described above.

Some readers may be thinking that this sounds suspiciously like the Brunswick stew popular in North Carolina counties east of Forsyth. Members of the Moravia Moravian congregation in Summerfield-Oak Ridge even have the big iron pot to cook it in over an open fire. Once a year they hold the "Community Stew" where friends and neighbors come in the morning and throw whatever they have into the pot, which cooks all day. Everyone then returns in the evening to enjoy the stew together. A very similar stew (complete with big iron pot) is also known in West Salem, Illinois (though they call it "chowder"). Perhaps North Carolina, Illinois, and South Africa are not so far apart after all!

The following is one of hundreds of ways of making potjiekos. In fact, anything you would prepare in a slow cooker is good for this. The recipe given here will feed more than four. How many more is up to you.

In your largest "potjie" or stewpot, bring one gallon of water up to a slow boil. Stir in whatever of the following you have available:

Cubes of beef, pork, lamb, rabbit, squirrel (not as popular as it used to be), to make about 3 lbs. in all. Add a whole cut-up chicken (with bones and skin, but discard giblets and trim off excess fat). Cook meats and chicken covered for about half an hour at a slow boil.

Then add 2 15-oz. cans each of tomatoes with juice, lima beans, corn, and 1 can green beans and 1 of green peas, etc., all drained. Add 4 or 5 potatoes, peeled and diced, along with 4 or 5 onions, diced. Some South African recipes also call for adding some pasta to the pot.

Season with salt and pepper, and a T. or so of rosemary or thyme or a mixture of both. Add 1 T. of garlic and several shakes of seasoned salt and Worcestershire sauce.

Cook for half an hour at a slow boil, then reduce heat, cover, and simmer slowly for another hour or more.

Fish the chicken pieces out, discard skin, remove meat from bone, shred, and return meat to pot.

Taste for seasonings, and add more if needed. Allow to simmer for a while more. Longer simmering, another hour or two, makes better stew.

Serve in large bowls with cornbread or rotis, which in this case are like flour tortillas, but see Caribbean section (page 100) for a leavened version. Provide a bottle of hot sauce for those who want to add it to their portion.

Note: This recipe requires a really large stew pot and feeds a lot of people. If you don't have that big a pot you can make a half recipe in a very large Dutch oven. However, this is one of those recipes that work best in large quantities. The purchase of a large pot and having over a large group of friends and relations is worth it. Any leftover stew freezes well.

Roast Chicken

Members returning from the Unity Band Festival reported that not only were the chickens in South Africa very flavorful, they were also huge! Roasting is a favorite way of preparing them. American chickens nowadays tend to be rather small. Find a good-size one if you can. I have noticed that Hispanic markets tend to have chickens more like what I remember from childhood as "a good-size roasting hen." The following is one suggestion for approximating the delicious South African roasted chicken.

1 whole chicken (4 lbs. or more)
salt and pepper to taste
3 T. vegetable oil
2 tsp. poultry seasoning, divided
3 oranges
3 lemons or limes
1 T. honey
½ cup orange juice

Remove neck, giblets, etc., from inside chicken and discard, or use later to make a gravy. Wash chicken well inside and out, and pat dry. Rub oil over the outside of the chicken, and sprinkle 1 tsp. poultry seasoning over the bird. Season with salt and pepper. Stuff cavity with quartered oranges and lemons (and/or limes).

Place chicken on rack in roasting pan, breast side up. Add 1 cup water in bottom and roast in preheated 350° oven for an hour or a little longer for a 4-pound bird. Add 10 or 15 minutes for a 5-pound one.

Baste every 10 minutes or so. You may want to cover the breast with tinfoil for part of the time so it doesn't burn or dry out. Add more water to pan as needed. For the last 10 minutes combine the remaining tsp. poultry seasoning with honey and orange juice, and paint on chicken with a pastry brush to give the skin a lovely color and flavor. Check for doneness by pricking thigh and seeing that the juices run clear. If not, cook 10 or 15 more minutes and check again.

South African Chicken Pie

During the 2007 Band Festival, Christo Appel of Cape Town provided a couple of recipes for chicken or game pie. This is a reasonable approximation and combination. Compare with the American version of chicken pie (page 68).

2 cups cubed or shredded cooked chicken	3 T. flour
4 slices bacon	1 cup chicken broth
1 small onion, diced	1½ cups milk (approx.)
½ cup button mushrooms	salt and pepper to taste
1 to 3 T. butter	pastry for 1 crust pie, or equal amount of puff pastry

Fry bacon until crisp, remove from pan, and reserve. Fry onions and mushrooms (whole buttons or sliced) in bacon grease. Add a little more oil if needed. Remove onions and mushrooms, and set aside. Add butter to remaining grease to make 3 T. Add flour and stir to make a roux. Stir in chicken broth and enough milk to make a medium thick white sauce. Check for seasoning, and add salt and pepper as needed. (Remember, bacon is already salty.)

Stir chicken, crumbled bacon, onions, and mushrooms into sauce, and put in deep-dish pie pan (no bottom crust). Cover top with regular pie crust or thawed puff pastry.

Brush top with a little milk, Cut a slit in regular pastry to release steam. Bake in a preheated 350° oven until top is nicely browned, 30 to 40 minutes usually.

Curried Chicken

Ray Gatland said that in his two weeks in South Africa he ate more curry than he had the rest of his life. "But I loved it," he assured me. This is a particularly easy and tasty example.

4 boneless, skinless chicken breasts	1 green chili (optional)
6 oz. plain yogurt	1 tsp. minced garlic
1 T. curry powder, divided	¼ tsp. ground turmeric
2 to 3 T. vegetable oil	¼ tsp. ground cinnamon
1 onion, sliced thin	¼ tsp. ground coriander
1 tomato, diced (optional)	1 cup chicken broth
	2 cups coconut milk

Cut chicken into bite-size cubes. Mix 1 tsp. curry powder with yogurt, spread over chicken, and leave to marinate in refrigerator for 30 minutes to an hour.

Heat 2 T. oil in heavy pan. Pat most of yogurt mixture off chicken pieces, and fry chicken in oil until nicely browned. Remove from pan and drain.

Add more oil to pan to make 2 T., and fry onion and tomato and chili (if used) until they begin to brown. Use the chili only if you like very hot curry. Add remaining 2 tsp. curry powder and garlic, turmeric, cinnamon, and coriander. Let cook for a few seconds, then add 1 cup chicken broth.

Reduce heat, and return chicken to pan. Cook for several minutes until chicken is done. Take out a piece and cut it. If center is still pink, return to pan and cook some more. Then check again.

Add coconut milk, and stir to blend until heated through. Serve over rice.

Note: Some curry powder can be rather hot, so the first time you make this you may want to add only a little at first, then taste at the end, and add more if you want. Remember too that family and friends may not like things as hot as you do. You can always make the dish mild, and provide hot sauce for those who want to spice it up.

Kudu
(Antelope)

When I first saw "kudu" listed as one of the favorite things eaten in South Africa, I thought it was a misprint. A word search revealed that, sure enough, it is a type of antelope.

Some antelope is grown commercially in the U.S., so you might be able to find it in a specialty market. Venison can be a substitute. A standard American cookbook says antelope is finer and less "gamy" than most other "hoofed game," and it somewhat resembles veal. So you might also use veal as a substitute.

Kudu is eaten as roasts, chops, and even burgers. To get some approximation of the flavor of kudu, take about 2 pounds of antelope or veal roast or chops and marinate for several hours in refrigerator in a solution of:

1 cup water
¼ cup vinegar
1 sliced onion or ½ tsp. onion powder
1 tsp. garlic, minced

1 tsp. rosemary
1 T. juniper berries
½ tsp. paprika
ground black pepper

Remove roast or chops from marinade, pat dry, and allow to come to room temperature.

For roast, cook uncovered in a preheated 350° oven for 20 minutes a pound for medium, and 25 minutes a pound for medium-well. Put some water or broth in the bottom of the pan at the start, and baste roast every 10 minutes or so. Add more liquid as it evaporates. Remove from oven, allow to rest for at least 15 minutes, and slice. Serve with gravy, a starch, and roast vegetables (page 178).

For chops, cook as you would a steak in a fairly hot pan for 4 to 6 minutes a side, depending on how thick they are and how done you prefer your meat. This would also work well as a "braii" (page 167) over wood, charcoal, or a gas grill outdoors.

Bobotie

Thanks again to Christo Appel of Cape Town for the basics of this combination meatloaf and quiche. Compare with the meatloaf in the American section (page 74).

2 lbs. ground beef or lamb	2 T. lemon or lime juice
2 slices stale white bread	1½ tsp. curry powder
1¼ cup milk, divided	1 tsp. turmeric
1 onion, diced	3 eggs
1 T. apricot jam	salt and pepper to taste
1 T. mango or other fruit chutney	

Toast bread and tear into small pieces. Soak in ¼ cup of the milk to soften. Then squeeze out most of milk, discard milk, and set bread aside.

Mix meat with onion, jam, chutney, lemon juice, curry, turmeric, and salt and pepper. Crumble mixture into frying pan, and cook until meat is browned and onion is tender. Put meat mixture into a casserole, or leave it in the pan if you used a heavy ovenproof one.

Beat the eggs into the remaining 1 cup milk with a little more salt and pepper. Pour eggs and milk over meat in casserole or pan.

Bake in a preheated 350° oven for 45 minutes to an hour until egg mixture is set and a little browned.

Serve with a salad, potatoes, and other vegetables.

Bredie

Christo Appel also graciously supplied the details of this versatile Cape Town favorite. In its most basic form, this is a simple meat-and-potato stew. With the suggested additions, it becomes a host of dishes.

2 lbs. lamb or beef stew meat
3 T. vegetable oil
2 onions, thinly sliced or diced
1 bell pepper, diced
2 large potatoes, peeled and cubed
salt and pepper to taste
1 cup beef broth
chili pepper or hot sauce (optional)

Fry cubes of meat in oil until they are lightly browned on all sides. Add onions and bell pepper and cook until softened but not browned.

Add potatoes, salt and pepper, and chopped chili or sauce. Stir for potatoes to pick up a little color. Add beef broth, reduce heat, cover, and simmer until meat is done and potatoes are tender. Serve over rice.

Additions: Before adding broth, stir in 3 or 4 chopped tomatoes with 1 tsp. basil, thyme, or marjoram. **Or** add 2 cups chopped cabbage or cauliflower with a stalk of thinly sliced celery and ¼ tsp. grated nutmeg. **Or** add green beans or lima beans with a little more salt and pepper. **Or** add 2 cups of your favorite squash, cubed, with a little sugar, nutmeg, and cinnamon.

Cauliflower in Curry Sauce

Curry is popular in South Africa with vegetables too. The following basic recipe can turn into several dishes with the addition of other vegetables as given below. Compare with the Tibetan recipe (page 224).

1 head cauliflower, trimmed and cut into pieces, or 2 (10 oz.) pkgs. frozen cauliflower
2 T. butter
2 tsp. flour
1 T. curry powder
1 cup milk
salt and pepper

Boil fresh cauliflower until softened but still a little firm, or cook frozen cauliflower according to package directions.

Melt butter in a pot or large saucepan. Add flour and cook over medium heat for 1 to 2 minutes. Add curry powder, stir, and cook for a minute more.

Add milk slowly, stirring to avoid lumps until you have a thickened sauce. Add salt and pepper to taste.

Add well-drained cooked cauliflower, and simmer for a few minutes.

Check for seasoning, and serve as a side dish or as a main dish over rice or potatoes.

Note: You can use less curry powder for a less hot flavor.

Variations: Add with cauliflower to curry sauce a cup (total) of one or more of the following cooked vegetables:

green peas
carrots
cubed potatoes
broccoli
chick peas (also called garbanzo beans or ceci)
green beans
lima beans

Roast Vegetables

This recalls European vegetable accompaniments for roast meat, though a South African description says they are great for a "braii" (page 167).

¼ cup vegetable oil
3 potatoes
2 or 3 onions
4 carrots
2 ribs celery

½ cup butternut squash
1 parsnip
salt and pepper to taste
garlic powder to taste

Place oil in a roasting pan in a preheated 350° oven and heat until shimmering hot.

As oil heats, peel a selection of the above vegetables (such as you have; omit what you don't), and cut into good-size cubes, 1 inch or a little bigger. Stir vegetables into pan to coat all sides with oil, and season as desired.

Bake uncovered in preheated 350° oven 45 minutes to an hour, turning occasionally until vegetables are tender inside and nicely browned on the outside.

Lentil Stew

Lentils make a tasty, healthy accompaniment to all sorts of meats, especially lamb. You can make them as spicy or mild as you like. Here are a couple possibilities.

½ cup dried lentils, any color
2 T. butter
½ onion, cubed
½ bell pepper, seeded and chopped
1 tomato, chopped (optional)
1 tsp. thyme
salt and pepper to taste
water as needed

Soak lentils in enough water to cover for an hour or two. Discard water and reserve lentils.

Melt butter in a large pot or Dutch oven, and fry onion and bell pepper until they begin to get a good brown color. Add lentils, tomato, thyme, and some salt and pepper. Lentils are naturally peppery, so watch the pepper. Add water to cover lentils by about an inch.

Bring to boil, then reduce heat, cover, and simmer for anywhere from a half hour to an hour or more until lentils are tender. Lentils have a mind of their own. They are done when they are done, so 45 minutes is a good guess. Stir occasionally. Add more water if pot begins to dry out.

Variations: If you like lentils spicy, add 1 T. curry powder and/or a hot chili in place of the thyme. Some folks like to add a washed and chopped leek in place of or in addition to the onion. If you prefer a thicker stew, use a potato masher or stick blender to mash some of the cooked lentils, and stir in to thicken liquid.

You can also add a pound of lamb or other stew meat or chicken to cook along with lentils. This turns the dish into a main course, giving you lamb- or beef-, pork-, kudu-, chicken-, etc., and-lentil stew.

Dumplings

As in many countries, dumplings of various sorts are appreciated with gravy, stews, and soups in South Africa. You can use the recipe from the European Continental section for "Potato Dumplings" (page 35) or from the North American section for "Chicken and Dumplings Version A" (page 72). Either might be recognized as "typically South African."

Note: I also saw a South African recipe for potato puffs that was very similar to the German "Kartoffelpuffer" (potato pancakes, page 33) given in the European Continental section. You could follow that basic recipe, and since these are "puffs" not "pancakes," just add 1 tsp. of baking powder as you mix the other ingredients, and you have another dish appreciated in South Africa.

Pap

This is the South African name for the cooked cornmeal and water dish, like Italian polenta, called "fungi" or "funghi" (page 99) in the Caribbean and "ugali" (page 187) in Tanzania. See those sections of this book for directions. Like its "cousins" in other provinces of the Moravian Unity, pap is widely served in South Africa as a starch instead of or in addition to rice and potatoes.

Orange Cake

This sponge or sheet cake is deceptively simple to make, but it is so good! I suppose you could stack and ice these as a layer cake, but one layer at a time is plenty rich enough.

Use your favorite yellow cake recipe with the finely chopped zest of one orange blended in. Or if time is a factor use a top quality boxed yellow cake mix with zest added.

Grease and flour a 9 x 13-inch pan or two 8- or 9-inch round cake pans. Pour in batter and bake according to recipe as a sheet cake or as two single layers.

This is the fun part. When cake is nearly done, put about 1 cup orange juice into a saucepan and begin to warm it. Put 1½ cup powdered sugar into a bowl and mix in enough orange juice (from the pan) a spoonful or two at a time to make a thick syrup. Stir this syrup into the remaining heated orange juice, and add a drop or two of vanilla extract. Let cool just a little.

When cake is done, cut oven off, remove cake, and with a large fork prick holes all over the top of the cake. Pour orange and sugar mixture slowly over top of cake, being sure it seeps down into the holes.

Put the cake back into the still-hot oven for 3 to 5 minutes more.

When the cake has cooled a bit, you can simply cut it into pieces and serve as is, or with a dusting of powdered sugar. Or to be really fancy let it cool more and garnish the top with dollops of whipped cream and mandarin orange slices.

Carrot Cake

Judging from the number of recipes I got for this, carrot cake must be a real favorite with many South Africans. This is a composite of several of them.

¾ cup sugar
¾ cup brown sugar
1¼ cups vegetable oil
4 eggs
2 cups cake flour
2 tsp. baking powder
1 tsp. baking soda

1 tsp. salt
2 tsp. cinnamon
1 tsp. ground cardamom
1 tsp. vanilla
2 cups grated carrots
½ cup chopped toasted walnuts

Preheat oven to 350°.

Cream sugars and oil. Add eggs one at a time, beating after each. Mix together dry ingredients in another bowl, and slowly mix into wet ingredients, about a third at a time. Stir in vanilla.

Stir in carrots and walnuts. (Shake carrots and nuts in a little flour first to keep them from sinking.)

Pour evenly into 2 greased and floured layer cake pans. Shake pans to release any large air bubbles, and bake in preheated 350° oven for about 45 to 50 minutes. Test for doneness with a toothpick or thin knife inserted into the center. If it comes out clean, the cake is done. If not, bake a few minutes more.

Let cakes cool for 10 minutes, then remove from pans and allow to cool completely.

Icing: Mix together 1 lb. powdered sugar, 1 stick softened margarine, 8 oz. softened cream cheese, and 2 tsp. vanilla. Spread generously on one cake layer, put second on top, and cover whole with remaining icing. Sprinkle top with more chopped walnuts if you like.

Fruit Bars

Apricots seem to be as popular in South Africa as they are in the Czech Republic, so they are a favorite for this recipe. Pineapple is a great favorite also. Peaches work well too.

For crust:

1¾ cup flour
½ cup butter, softened

3 to 4 T. powdered sugar
pinch of salt

Mix all crust ingredients and press evenly into the bottom of a greased 9 x 12-inch ovenproof pan. If dough is too stiff to spread well, add a tsp. or so of water. Bake in a preheated 350° oven for 20 to 25 minutes or until crust has a nice golden brown color. Leave oven on.

For Fruit Topping:

2 (15 oz.) cans fruit, drained
4 T. flour
½ cup brown sugar
2 eggs
½ tsp. baking powder

¼ tsp. cinnamon
pinch of salt
1 tsp. vanilla
2 tsp. lemon juice
4 T. chopped toasted walnuts
powdered sugar (for garnish)

Chop the fruit and set aside.

Cream eggs and brown sugar, and then mix in the dry and other ingredients. Stir in fruit.

Spread evenly on cooked crust in pan, and bake about 20 to 25 minutes in the already hot 350° oven. If topping is still runny, bake a few minutes more.

Cool, sprinkle with a little powdered sugar, cut into 12 or more bars, and enjoy.

Tanzania

Moravian work in Tanzania began in 1889. Because of World War I and several financial crises, it looked for a time as if the work would have to be given up. We are fortunate that our Unity decided to hang on, however, for today there are four provinces of our church in Tanzania, and half of the Moravians in the world live in this country. And this former mission work is now actively engaged in mission work of its own, both within Tanzania and in Congo, Malawi, and Zambia.

Within this large country, there are obviously regional differences in the cuisine. In general, Tanzanian cooking is firmly based in its African roots, enriched by influences brought in through extensive trade with India, Arabia, and elsewhere. Bananas, coconuts, and peanuts provide favorite flavors.

Chapatti Bread

In Tanzania this bread, originally from India, is a standard starch accompaniment to all sorts of dishes. In fact, though, it is almost exactly like a Mexican flour tortilla. You can make it yourself, and some people recommend this for a fresher flavor. If you want to do that, consult any number of Indian or Mexican cookbooks.

Given the time and effort involved, however, I advise going to an Indian market and buying ready-made chapatti, or picking up a pack of Mexican flour tortillas (whole-wheat if you can find them) in your local supermarket.

To prepare, warm in a microwave for 30 seconds, or fry in a pan with butter and oil for 30 seconds a side. Cover, and keep warm in a 200° oven or in a microwave, and serve when needed.

Meat Sambusas

The basic recipe for these little meat pie snacks was brought back from Tanzania several years ago by Moravian minister Steve Craver. I already had the first thoughts for a cookbook such as this, and when I heard Steve was going, I asked him to get a few recipes for me. He graciously complied, and we can all be glad he did.

Filling:

4 oz. ground meat
½ cup onion, finely chopped
2 tsp. garlic, chopped
½ tsp. ground cardamom

2 chilies, chopped
1 T. coriander (cilantro) leaves, chopped
salt to taste

Cook meat, onions, and garlic with salt and seasonings. Drain well and allow to cool.

The original recipe has directions for making a dough to contain the filling. Since this comes out almost exactly like commercially prepared egg roll wrappers, I suggest using those.

Take a wrapper and cut in half diagonally to make two triangles. Make cones of each half, having the point at the bottom, and the long side at the top. Moisten fingers with a little water and squeeze edges so they stick together, leaving top open. Place a good heaping T. of filling in each, and squeeze top edges to seal. Repeat until filling is used up.

Fry in hot oil until golden brown all around. Drain and serve with lemon wedges.

Note: The recipe as brought back by Br. Craver, calls for "1 bundle kotimiri" in the filling. I had no idea what that was. Thanks to search engines on the Internet, I now know that it is coriander leaves, also known as cilantro. I'm still not sure how big a "bundle" is, but you can take my guess as to a suitable amount, or do less or more as you think best.

Ugali

This polenta-like dish is a usual accompaniment to other dishes. It is usually made rather thick and firm enough to roll into balls. Basically, it is corn or other similar meal boiled in water. Recipes, though, have many variations as to ratio of meal to water, how much of each to add when, and whether to add salt. The following method is simple and works well.

Stir 1 cup cornmeal (white works best) and 1 tsp. salt into 2 cups water, and continue to stir as you bring it just to a boil. Be careful: if it gets too hot and forms big bubbles, they can pop and burn you. Lift off heat, reduce heat to simmer, and continue to stir while burner cools down. After a couple of minutes, return pot to heat. Stir often until meal is cooked and mixture is very thick and hard to stir. Let cool and serve by spoonfuls or shape into about 8 balls.

I have also made ugali using farina instead of cornmeal. This cooks quickly and stiffens up almost immediately after coming to a boil. It makes, in effect, "instant ugali." The cooked product will be a little softer than that made with cornmeal, however.

Tanzanian Curry Powder

Many Tanzanian dishes call for curry powder. We know that "curry" as used here is not a single spice or herb, but is a mixture of many.

Curry powder is from India originally, and is usually reddish in the north and yellow in the south of that country.

The favorite kind in much of Tanzania is orange in color. You can get a good approximation of this simply by mixing yellow curry powder, readily available almost everywhere, with an equal amount of Indian red tandoori masala or garam masala, available in some grocery stores and specialty markets. The resulting mixture is rather hot, so use sparingly if you don't like your dishes too spicy.

Several of the following recipes call for curry powder, but you can also simply use this in your own recipes to season meat, poultry, or fish before grilling, frying, etc.

Braised Fish

When it is available, fish is popular among Moravians in Tanzania. Generally, the preference is to fry the fish first, and then add it to sauces, stews, soups, etc. The following is an example of characteristic flavors. Breading the fish before frying is an optional embellishment, but it does soak up the flavors nicely later.

4 fish filets	1 tsp. garlic, chopped
salt and pepper to taste	1 tsp. to 1 T. curry powder
½ cup flour or cornmeal	1 tomato, chopped
3 T. vegetable oil	1 cup fish broth
1 onion, sliced	1 banana (optional)
1 bell pepper, sliced	crushed roasted peanuts

Salt and pepper fish, and place in zip-top plastic bag with flour or cornmeal. Shake to coat fish. Remove fish from bag, shake off excess coating, and fry in 2 T. oil until nicely brown. Remove and set aside.

In same pan, add more oil to make about 2 T. Add onions, bell peppers, and garlic, and cook for a couple of minutes. Add curry powder, and cook for a minute or so more. Add tomato and fish broth (bottled clam juice from the market works fine). Simmer to blend flavors. Add peeled and thickly sliced banana here. Put fish back in pan, and turn to coat in sauce. Simmer just a minute and serve over rice. Garnish with crushed peanuts.

Chicken in Coconut Milk

The original of this recipe may have come from the island of Madagascar, but its ingredients and cooking method are typical of East Africa in general, including Tanzania.

4 pieces of chicken (your choice)
¼ cup lemon or lime juice
½ tsp. fresh grated ginger
½ tsp. garlic, chopped
pepper sauce

3 T. vegetable oil
1 onion, diced
1 tomato, diced
1 cup coconut milk

Put chicken in a zip-top plastic bag with juice, ginger, garlic, and pepper sauce to taste (depending on how hot you want the end result to be), and let the chicken marinate for an hour or more. Remove chicken, and discard marinade.

Heat oil in frying pan, and brown chicken on all sides. Add diced onion, and fry until it begins to brown too. Add tomato and fry for a couple minutes more. You can also add more ginger and/or garlic at this point if you wish.

Add ½ cup water to the pan, reduce heat, cover, and cook for 20 minutes. Add more water if pan begins to go dry during this time.

Then remove lid, and let most of the water evaporate. Add coconut milk, stir, and simmer for 10 minutes. Check that chicken is done. Add more seasoning if needed, and serve with rice and/or ugali (page 187).

Variation: A curried version of this called "kuku paka" is popular also. Proceed as above, but fry ½ sliced or diced bell pepper with the onion, and add 1 tsp. Tanzanian curry powder (page 188) and a dash of ground cloves as they brown.

Chicken in Cumin Sauce

4 pieces of chicken (your choice)
3 T. vegetable oil
1 onion, diced
1 tsp. garlic, minced

1 cup tomato sauce
1 tsp. ground cumin
hot chili or pepper sauce
salt and pepper to taste

Fry chicken in oil until lightly browned but not fully cooked. Remove from pan and set aside.

Fry onion in oil chicken was browned in until it begins to brown. Add garlic, stir, and cook a minute more.

Add tomato sauce, cumin, diced chili or pepper sauce to taste. Salt and pepper as needed.

Return chicken to pan, reduce heat, cover, and simmer 30 to 40 minutes. Add water if sauce gets too thick during cooking. Check a piece to be sure chicken is done through. Serve with rice or other starch.

Variations: The above can be made with 1 pound of cubed stewing beef, pork, or lamb instead of chicken.

Chicken with Groundnuts and Tomato

"Groundnuts" is a popular name for peanuts in Tanzania. For this dish prepare the above recipe, but omit cumin. During last 10 minutes or so of cooking, put ¼ cup finely ground roasted peanuts or 2 T. peanut butter in a cup, stir in some tomato sauce from the pan to dissolve, and pour back to mix with sauce in pan.

Pepper Sauce Chicken
(Piri-Piri)

This and similar dishes developed after the Portuguese brought new kinds of hot chili peppers from the Americas to Africa. A similar dish made its way then to Portugal, where it became so popular it is claimed as a national dish. It is still well liked in many parts of East Africa.

4 pieces of chicken (your choice)
4 T. vegetable oil
½ cup lemon juice or cider vinegar
½ tsp. fresh grated ginger
1 tsp. garlic, chopped
½ tsp. ground coriander

½ tsp. ground cinnamon
½ tsp. dried marjoram
1 tsp. paprika
½ to 2 chopped hot chilies
or
½ to 2 tsp. red pepper sauce

In a large measuring cup or similar container combine all ingredients except chicken. The original is very hot, but you may tone it down by using less chili or pepper sauce. Stir to mix well, or puree in electric blender.

Pour about ⅔ of the mixture into a zip-top plastic bag, and put chicken in to marinate for an hour or so. Reserve rest of mixture to brush on chicken as it cooks (thus avoiding contamination).

Remove chicken from bag and pat dry. Discard marinade.

Cook chicken on a hot grill until it has brown grill marks on all sides. Reduce heat a little, and brush with some of the reserved sauce. Continue cooking, turning, and brushing with more sauce until chicken is done. This may take 15 to 30 minutes total, depending on what cut of chicken you use. Check for doneness just to be sure.

Serve with rice or potatoes and a vegetable (pages 196-202).

Tanzanian Flavored Fried Chicken

The following is a combination of traditional fried chicken with a strong Tanzanian flavor. You will definitely think of Tanzania each time you enjoy this dish.

4 pieces chicken (your choice)
1 cup buttermilk or plain yogurt
1 T. Tanzanian curry powder
   (page 188)
½ tsp. fresh ginger
¼ tsp. ground cumin
½ tsp. garlic powder
½ tsp. onion powder
salt to taste
1 cup flour
oil for frying

Mix buttermilk or yogurt with curry powder, ginger, cumin, garlic, and onion in a zip-top plastic bag. Add chicken and let marinate for an hour or more.

In another bag mix flour and salt. You can also add another shake or two of some of the seasonings to the flour if you want.

Remove chicken from marinade, discard marinade, and put wet pieces into the bag of seasoned flour. Shake to coat well.

Shake off excess flour, and fry chicken in hot oil (not too hot) until crust is nice and brown. Check for doneness and serve.

Meat Stew

In essence, you can make your favorite stew, just adding some typical Tanzanian seasonings. The following is an example.

1 lb. cubed beef, lamb, or pork stew meat
2 T. vegetable oil
½ cup onions, chopped
2 tsp. garlic, chopped
salt and pepper to taste
1 T. Tanzanian curry powder (page 188)
1 tsp. ground cinnamon
2 potatoes, peeled and cubed
2 cups mixed carrots, celery, bell peppers, cubed
2 T. flour
1 (15 oz.) can tomatoes
2 cups beef or chicken broth
1 cup coconut milk

Cook meat cubes in oil until they have browned a little. Add onions, garlic, salt and pepper, stir, and cook a couple of minutes more. Add curry powder and cinnamon, and stir. (You can use 1 tsp. each of ground cardamom, ground coriander, and turmeric instead of curry powder if you prefer.)

Add potatoes and vegetables, and cook a couple minutes until they have taken on a good color. Add flour and stir to mix well. Add tomatoes with a little of their juice, broth, and coconut milk. Simmer about 20 minutes to a half hour until meat and vegetables are done.

Garnish with a little shredded coconut and crushed peanuts if you like.

Note: Some versions omit the coconut milk and add more broth. Other versions add a peeled and thick sliced plantain to cook with the vegetables. Instead of plantain, you can add a sliced banana for the last 5 minutes of simmering.

Note also: There is no law that says you can't use chicken instead of the other meats for the above dish.

Tanzanian Roast Meat

Simply cook your favorite roast of beef, pork, or lamb as you normally would, but give it a dry rub first of Tanzanian curry powder (page 188) and some garlic and onion powder. Letting it sit an hour or two before roasting helps the flavor.

Tanzanian Beans and Rice

Like ugali, rice and beans is a staple starch side dish in Tanzania, and sometimes is the main course. Compare with Central American recipes (pages 140-143). Indeed, the Caribbean versions are descended from those of Africa, adapted to ingredients available locally. This basic dish is common throughout much of Africa, but the following is a Tanzanian variation incorporating the favorite flavor of coconut.

The cumin is listed as optional since some find it overpowers the other seasonings. Try it both ways and decide for yourself. Either way, this is really good!

3 T. butter or oil
½ onion, sliced thin
1 bell pepper, sliced thin
¾ tsp. Tanzanian curry powder
1 tsp. garlic powder
½ tsp. ground coriander

pinch to ¼ tsp. cumin (optional)
1 cup rice
½ to ¾ tsp. salt
1¾ cup water
¾ cup coconut milk, divided
1 (15 oz.) can kidney beans

Heat oil or butter (or mixture), and add onion and bell pepper (use green, red, yellow, or mixture for color). Stir, and add curry powder, garlic powder, coriander, and cumin. Stir until onion and peppers just begin to soften. Remove onion and peppers, and set aside. Add a little more butter or oil to pan if needed to make 2 T.

Add rice and stir to coat in seasoned oil. Cook 1 to 2 minutes. Add salt, then pour in water and ½ cup of the coconut milk. Stir to blend. Reduce heat to simmer, cover pan, and let rice steam for 20 minutes.

Add remaining coconut milk. Rinse kidney beans, add to pot, and stir. Add reserved onion and bell peppers. Stir, and simmer for 3 to 5 minutes more. Check for salt, and serve with meat, poultry, fish, or vegetables.

Note: Instead of kidney beans, you can use canned pintos, black-eyed peas, or crowder peas. All of these approximate local Tanzanian beans or peas commonly used as available.

Spinach with Groundnuts (Peanuts)

This is another recipe brought back by Steve Craver. It makes a good side dish or sauce with other vegetables and meats.

1 lb. spinach
1 large tomato
1 large onion
2 or 3 cloves garlic
1 tsp. turmeric
1 or 2 chilies
1 cup water or vegetable stock
½ cup groundnuts (peanuts), roasted and finely ground

Blanch tomato in hot water for 2 minutes or so. Peel and chop. Finely slice onion, chilies, and garlic. Put tomato, onion, garlic, turmeric, and chili in a pan and simmer, covered, over low heat.

As the above simmers, remove stalks from spinach and wash thoroughly. Blanch spinach in boiling water for 10 seconds. Remove and chop finely. (Or you can cook a 10 oz. box of frozen chopped spinach. Just be sure to thaw and squeeze out most of the water.)

Mix the groundnuts with the water or stock. Add this mixture to the tomato mixture and continue to simmer.

Add spinach to cooking mixture and continue to simmer for another 5 to 10 minutes. Salt and pepper to taste.

Serve hot as a vegetable or sauce.

Note: Ready made peanut butter (smooth or chunky) can be substituted for the groundnuts (though it really doesn't work as well). If you go with this option, use only 1 to 2 T. peanut butter.

Greens and Potatoes

Similar dishes are common throughout Eastern and Southern Africa. Compare also to the Dutch potatoes and cabbage (page 37) in the European section.

1 lb. kale, spinach, or Swiss chard, etc., or 1 (10 oz.) box, frozen
2 large potatoes
1 cup chicken broth
¼ tsp. ground nutmeg
salt and pepper to taste

Chop fresh greens into small pieces. If using frozen, get already chopped ones if you can. Cook greens in chicken broth until tender, up to a half hour.

Peel and cube potatoes. Cook in salted water for 20 minutes or until tender. Drain, and mash. Add some salt and pepper. Some folks like to add a little butter also. Add ¼ cup or so of the chicken broth in which the greens were cooked to thin potatoes to a moderately soft consistency.

Mix drained greens into potatoes, and add nutmeg. Check for seasoning, and serve with fish or meat dishes.

Braised Cabbage

This is a simple dish but a tasty and pretty one. This is a lot like the braised cabbage (page 15) in the Czech section, only this has a Tanzanian flair. The curry powder gives this a slow but increasing burn, so use a little, taste, and then add more if you want.

2 T. vegetable oil
½ cup onions, chopped
1 medium or ½ large head white or green cabbage
1 or 2 tsp. Tanzanian curry powder

½ tsp. salt
2 tsp. flour
1 T. lemon juice
1 tsp. sugar

In a large Dutch oven heat oil over medium heat. Add onions and cook until soft but not browned. Cut cabbage into thin strips and add to oil with curry powder and salt. Pour in ½ cup water and braise, covered, for 20 minutes. Stir occasionally and add a little more water if pot is going dry. Sprinkle on flour and cook 5 minutes more. Add lemon juice and sugar. Stir, check for seasoning, and serve with rice, meat, or fish.

Note: If you want the color but not the flavor of the curry, use 1 or 2 tsp. turmeric in place of the curry powder.

Tanzanian Succotash

In its simplest form, this is simply corn and dried beans cooked together. It is much the same as githeri or irio from different regions of nearby Kenya.

For the basic recipe, simply cook a 15 oz. can of corn (not cream style) with one of kidney, pinto, etc., beans, or black-eyed, field, or crowder peas.

Some variations add lima beans and/or spinach, or other greens and/or potatoes. Do whatever sounds good. For a deluxe version, you can also add some crisply fried thin sliced onion.

Eggplant with Curry
(Mchuzi wa Biringani)

1 medium eggplant	1 tsp. Tanzanian curry powder
4 T. vegetable oil	1 tsp. sugar
1 onion, diced	1 cup coconut milk
1 tsp. garlic, chopped	salt and pepper to taste

Fry onion in oil until it begins to brown. Add garlic and cook for a minute more. Add curry powder and sugar, and stir to mix.

Cut eggplant (peeled or not as you prefer) into good-size cubes, and add to onion-curry mixture. Fry until eggplant takes on a good color. Add a little water if pot is dry, reduce heat, cover, and simmer for 12 to 15 minutes.

Add coconut milk, stir, and heat until warm. Add salt and pepper to taste. Serve as side dish to meat or fish with chapatti bread and rice.

Variation: You can marinate the eggplant in yogurt, cover in flour or breadcrumbs, and deep fry before adding to onion-curry mixture. It will not need to simmer as long before adding the coconut milk.

Stir Fry Vegetables
(with accompaniments)

Thanks are again due to Steve Craver for bringing this recipe, which is designed to encourage variations. You can make at least a dozen different dishes in fact.

6 oz. cabbage, shredded
6 oz. cucumber, diced
3 oz. lettuce, shredded
6 oz. carrots, coarsely grated
6 oz. tomatoes, chopped
3 oz. bell pepper, chopped
2 oz. spinach, coarsely chopped

2 or 3 T. vegetable oil
1 cup or more water
salt to taste

4 to 6 oz. lean beef
or
4 to 6 oz. chicken
or
4 to 6 oz. fish steak
or
2 or 3 eggs

2 tsp. cornstarch
2 T. soy sauce

Choose at least 2 or 3 of the vegetables, as available. More is better, though using them all might be a bit excessive.

Cut meat, poultry, or fish into small pieces, preferably thin strips or cubes. Precook meat, etc., by boiling or frying. If eggs are used, scramble, or hard boil and chop.

Heat oil in a deep frying pan. Fry the hardest vegetables first: i.e., carrots, then cabbage, then bell pepper, etc. Then add the rest so that the softest (spinach or lettuce) are put in last.

When vegetables have cooked a little but are still firm, add water and simmer for a minute or two.

Mix cornstarch with a little water into a smooth paste. Add soy sauce and stir this mixture into the vegetables.

Add meat, poultry, fish, or eggs. You can add additional seasoning at this point (see note below).

Continue cooking until sauce thickens and vegetables are cooked but still a little crunchy. Add more water if sauce gets too thick.

Add salt to taste (remember, soy sauce is salty) and serve immediately with rice or ugali (page 187) and/or chapatti (page 185).

Note: You can also mix the meats, poultry, and fish as you do the vegetables to make even more variations. Also if you like more seasoning, add garlic powder, dried pepper flakes, chopped coriander leaves (cilantro), ginger, or ground cardamom, etc., when you add the meat, etc., to the vegetables.

Rice Doughnuts

Thanks again to Steve Craver for this recipe.

½ cup flour
2 cups rice flour
½ tsp. ground cinnamon
½ cup sugar, divided

1 (½ oz.) pkg. dry yeast
¼ cup milk for creaming yeast
1 cup water (approx.)
vegetable oil for shallow frying

Add cinnamon to flour and rice flour, sift into a large mixing bowl, and add sugar (reserving 1 tsp.).

Mix yeast, the 1 tsp. sugar, and warm milk, and leave to work until foamy.

Warm the water and stir into flour mixture to make a thick batter (like a very thick pancake batter). Add yeast mixture and a little more water if the batter is still too thick. Leave in a warm place "until it rises and produces a lot of air bubbles."

Heat about ½ inch oil to medium high heat in a large frying pan. Fry the batter by spoonfuls (a large dessert or soup spoon seems about right). Spread it out a little to form a good shape and even thickness.

Cook on both sides until cooked through and a light golden brown. Remove them from oil when you think they should be just a little browner (they darken more as they cool).

Remove from pan, drain, and roll in granulated or powdered sugar if desired.

This makes a couple dozen to "serve for snacks or packed meals." Compare this with the version given in the North India and Nepal section (page 227).

Favorite Flavors Banana Dessert

We have mentioned that bananas, coconuts, and peanuts are favorites in Tanzania. Curry is also well liked. This simple dessert brings them all together.

Melt 2 T. butter in pan and add a couple shakes of Tanzanian curry powder. Peel 2 bananas and cut longwise, and then crosswise into 4 or 6 pieces each. Fry pieces in the butter for just a minute or so a side. Remove from pan and sprinkle with shredded coconut and crushed roasted peanuts.

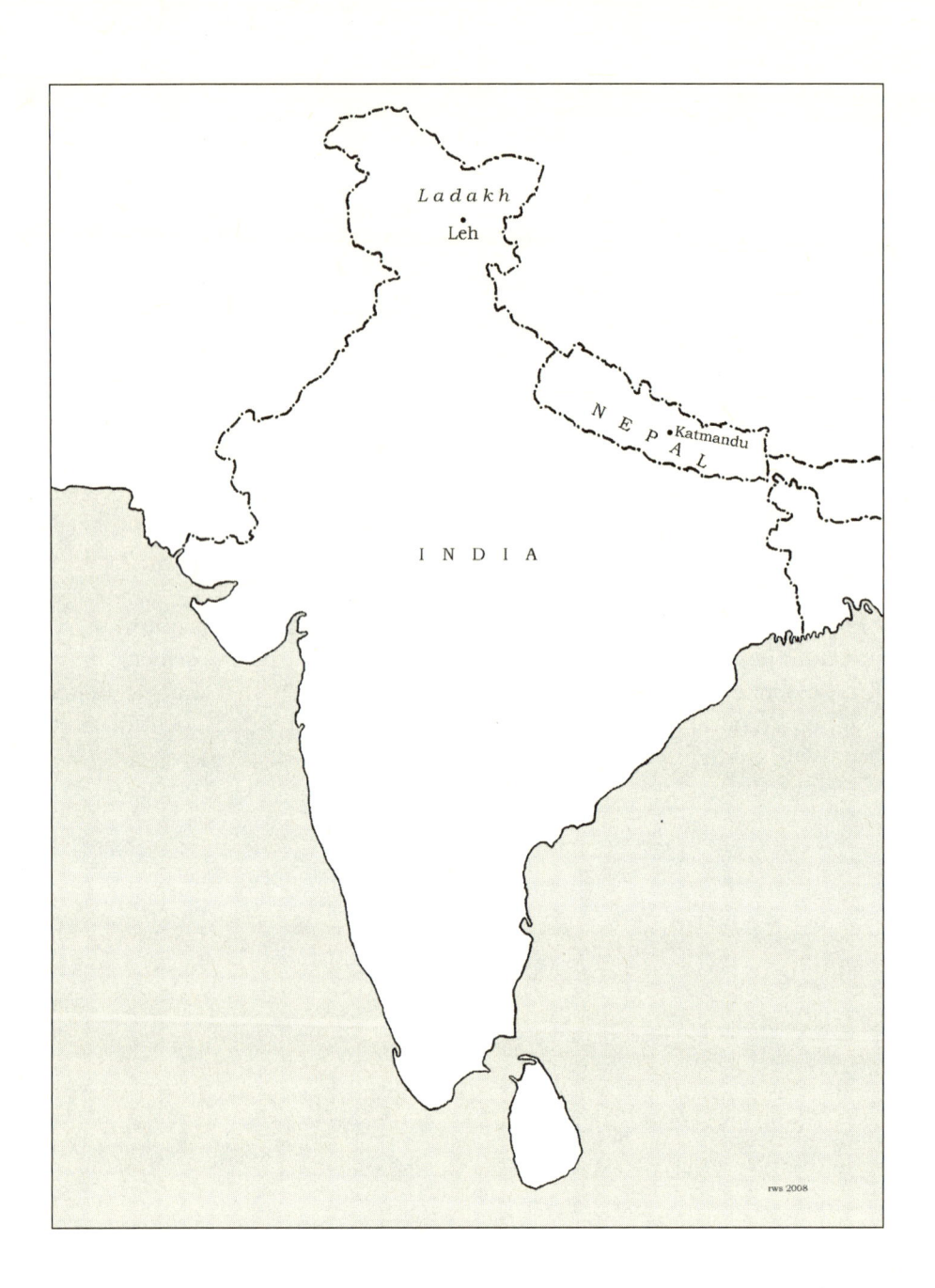

North India and Nepal

For years people spoke of "the Tibetan mission." In fact, for political reasons, Moravian workers were never allowed in Tibet itself, but from the 1850s have ministered among people of Tibetan extraction in northern India. The membership has always been small, but our church has engaged in educational and medical work among people of all faiths in the region.

Soon after 2000, a group of Christians from nearby Nepal approached the Moravian Church about becoming a part of our church. Christians are a very small minority in Nepal, and these young Christians felt the need of closer ties with Christians in other lands. They had heard about the Moravians' long mission heritage and gentle ways, and thought us an appropriate church to join. Already their work in music training for church workers is becoming a pattern for similar work in other provinces.

The cuisines of northern India and Nepal are naturally very close to each other with Tibetan and Chinese influence. It is light and tasty as well as spicy at times.

Vegetable Soup

1½ cups diced mixed vegetables
1 onion, diced
1 tsp. garlic
2 tsp. butter

1 cup tomato juice
2 cups broth
cheese for grating
salt and pepper to taste

Boil fresh vegetables in water until tender, or use canned or microwaved frozen ones. Drain, and put into food mill or blender. Lightly cook onion and garlic in the butter. Add to vegetables. Process until very smooth. (If using blender, you may need to add several T. of the tomato juice to get vegetables smooth.)

Put vegetable mixture into pot with tomato juice and broth (vegetable or chicken). Heat just to boil. Reduce heat, and grate in ½ to ¾ cup of cheese — Parmesan, Muenster, etc., as you please. Stir to blend. Check seasoning and serve in bowls.

If you prefer thinner soup, add some water or broth.

Tomato Soup

Compare this simple version with the more elaborate version in the Great Britain section (page 46). They are both very good.

6 tomatoes, chopped	¼ to ½ tsp. ground cumin
3 T. butter	2 cups water or chicken broth
1 onion, diced	pinch of sugar
salt and pepper to taste	1 cup cooked rice

Fry onion in butter until softened. Add tomatoes, salt and pepper, and cumin, and cook for 3 to 5 minutes.

Puree onion, tomato, and seasonings mixture in blender, and place in pot with water or broth and sugar. Stir well and bring to boil. Reduce heat. Stir in rice. Serve in bowls with basil or cilantro garnish on top.

Nepalese Onion Rings

These uniquely seasoned onion rings are a favorite snack, or can accompany other dishes in a meal.

1 large onion, cut in rings	salt to taste
1 jalapeño pepper	1 cup flour
¾ tsp. fresh ginger	1 T. vegetable oil
¾ tsp. ground cumin	½ to ¾ cup water (approx.)

Chop pepper and ginger fine. Add with cumin and salt to flour. Stir in 1 T. oil and enough water to make a thick batter. Dip onion rings in batter, shake off excess, and fry in hot oil until golden brown. Drain, salt lightly, and serve.

Onion and Tomato Salad

This can be eaten as a salad at the beginning of a meal or used with other sides to accompany main dishes.

1 tomato	1 tsp. cilantro or basil
½ onion	½ cup plain yogurt
¼ English cucumber	salt and pepper to taste

Chop or thinly slice tomato, onion, and cucumber. Cut cilantro or basil into thin strips.

Combine all ingredients, including yogurt, in a bowl, and refrigerate for at least a half hour to let flavors blend. Check for seasoning and serve in small individual bowls.

Tomato Achar

Achars are basically relishes used to accompany other dishes in a meal. They are made with various vegetables and fruits, and are generally quite spicy. You can tone down the heat if you need to. Tomato achar is particularly popular and makes an appearance with most meals.

¾ cup tomato sauce
½ tsp. fresh ginger
½ tsp. onion powder
½ tsp. garlic powder
1 jalapeño or serrano pepper
¼ tsp. salt
¼ tsp. dry mustard powder
1 T. vegetable oil
½ tsp. cilantro or basil

Use less or more hot pepper or hot sauce as you like. You can always add more later.

Mix all ingredients except cilantro or basil in saucepan, and cook gently until thickened to the consistency of medium-thin catsup. If achar tastes too acidic, add a pinch of sugar. Cool before serving with thinly cut cilantro or basil on top.

Mango Achar

Mangoes are also popular as a main ingredient in achars. Other fruits such as plums or peaches can be used also. Original recipes assume fresh fruits, but canned or frozen work well also.

Use ⅔ cup mango chopped into small pieces. Add ½ tsp. each fresh chopped ginger, onion powder, and garlic powder, with hot pepper as desired. Mix in ¼ tsp. each of salt, dry mustard, and turmeric. Add 1 T. vegetable oil, stir, and refrigerate (do not cook). You can garnish achar with fresh mint before serving.

Vegetable or Meat Samosas

Little fried pies like these appear in almost every cuisine worldwide. (See the Nicaragua, South Africa, and Tanzania sections for other examples, pages, 130, 158, 186.) The seasonings set these apart.

Dough:

1½ cup flour	2 T. butter
¼ tsp. salt	water

Mix flour and salt, and work in butter with your fingers. Add enough water (about ½ cup usually) to make a firm dough. Knead the dough for a couple minutes. (If the dough becomes sticky during kneading, dust on a little more flour.) You can also use commercial pie dough, but not the frozen preformed kind in pan. Set aside.

Vegetable Filling:

2 T. butter	2 T. canned green peas or peas
½ small onion, finely diced	and carrots
1 small cooked potato, finely diced	Pinch each of ground dried coriander, turmeric, paprika, garam masala, salt, pepper

Fry onion in butter until lightly browned. Add spices and salt and pepper to taste.

Add potato, peas, etc., and stir for a couple minutes. Check the seasoning, and cook until warmed through. Set aside to cool.

Meat Filling:

Fry ¼ lb. crumbled hamburger with half a diced onion. Drain grease from hamburger and add seasonings listed above for vegetable filling. Set aside to cool.

Assembly:

Knead dough again and divide into 8 pieces. On a floured surface roll out dough into thin circles or squares.

Put a T. or so of filling on each piece of dough, and fold over to make a half moon or triangle. Crimp edges with a fork to seal.

Fry in ½ inch of hot oil until golden brown on all sides. Remove from oil, drain, sprinkle with a little salt, and serve as appetizers or first course with achars, etc. (see above).

Note: If you prefer smaller samosas, just make the dough pieces smaller and put less filling in each.

Nepalese Fish Fry

These regions are far from the sea, but fresh water fish, when available, is a popular dish.

4 fish filets (trout, catfish, etc.)	¼ cup flour
1 onion, grated fine	1 egg, beaten
½ tsp. grated fresh ginger	½ cup breadcrumbs
2 tsp. lemon or lime juice	salt and pepper

Marinate fish for a half hour in onion, ginger, and lemon or lime juice. Pat mostly dry and sprinkle well with flour. Dip in egg and coat with breadcrumbs. Fry in hot oil for 5 minutes or so a side until golden brown. Salt and pepper to taste. Serve with lemon or lime wedges. Mango achar is particularly good with this.

Chicken Curry

2 boneless, skinless chicken breasts	salt and pepper to taste
1 onion, finely sliced	1 jalapeño or serrano chili
3 T. butter	1 T. garlic, minced
½ tsp. turmeric	½ tsp. fresh ginger
2 tsp. ground coriander	1 tsp. garam masala
½ tsp. ground cumin	1 cup water or broth

Fry onion in butter until it begins to brown. Some recipes say to grind turmeric, coriander, cumin, and salt and pepper with chili, garlic, and ginger to make a paste, and then add garam masala. I find it just as good to remove pan from heat, and add all spices without the paste step.

Cook spice mixture with onions in pan for a minute or two, then add the water or broth.

Cut chicken into bite-size cubes, add to pan, and cook for 10 to 12 minutes or until chicken is done.

Serve with rice, and garnish with lemon wedges and chopped parsley or cilantro.

Spinach and Chicken

Nola Knouse tells me this was a favorite of representatives of the American Mission Board who were visiting Nepal to learn about the Christian musicians' training school there.

4 pieces of chicken (your choice)
3 T. butter
1 onion, diced
1 T. garlic, minced
1 tsp. ground coriander

¼ tsp. ground cloves
½ tsp. ground cinnamon
1 cup water or broth
10 oz. cooked spinach
salt and pepper to taste

Fry onion pieces in butter until they begin to brown. Add garlic, stir, and fry for a minute more.

Add coriander, cloves, and cinnamon, and stir until they become fragrant.

Add chicken pieces and fry until they get a nice color. Add the water or chicken broth, and simmer until chicken is done. This will depend on what pieces you use: 12 minutes to a half hour or more.

Stir in spinach. Simmer until heated through, salt and pepper to taste, check other seasoning, adding more if you wish, and serve with rice or dumplings (page 220).

Meat Curry

If curries are popular in Suriname, South Africa, and Tanzania, imagine how popular they are in the lands of their origin.

1½ lbs. pork, lamb, or goat	3 T. butter
2 tsp. garam masala	1 onion, diced
1 tsp. ground cinnamon	1 T. garlic, minced
½ tsp. ground cumin	½ tsp. fresh ginger
¼ tsp. ground nutmeg	2 cups meat broth
½ cup plain yogurt	salt and pepper to taste

Cut meat into cubes. Mix spices with yogurt and rub over meat. Leave to marinate for an hour or so.

Fry onion in butter until it begins to brown, then add garlic and ginger. Stir and fry for a minute more.

Add meat with marinade to fry pan. Stir and let sizzle for a minute or two.

Add broth and simmer, covered, stirring occasionally until meat is done (20 to 30 minutes). Check for seasonings.

Serve with rice, dumplings, or potatoes, other vegetables, and achar (page 211).

Stuffed Bell Peppers

This is another local dish enjoyed by American Mission Board representatives in Nepal.

4 bell peppers (color of choice)	2 cooked potatoes, cubed
3 T. butter	¼ cup cooked green peas
1 small onion, diced	¼ cup sliced cooked carrots
2 tsp. garlic, minced	¼ cup cut cooked green beans
½ tsp. fresh ginger	1 tsp. flour
½ tsp. ground coriander	salt and pepper to taste
1 tsp. garam masala	¼ cup water (or more)

Hollow out bell peppers by removing stem, seeds, and veins. Set aside.

Fry onion pieces in butter until they begin to brown. Add garlic and ginger, and fry a minute more. Stir in spices until they become fragrant.

Add vegetables (canned vegetables work fine), stir, and cook until heated through. Sprinkle on flour, stir, and cook for a minute or so. Salt and pepper to taste. Add a little water to make a sauce to bind mixture together. Cool for 15 minutes.

Stuff vegetable mixture into hollowed-out bell peppers.

These can be baked in a preheated 350° oven for about a half hour until peppers are softened. Put them in a baking pan with a little water in the bottom. Add water as needed if pan starts to dry out.

They can also be cooked in a bamboo steamer, or even fried in oil until pepper skins get crispy. Serve as a side dish with meat or as a main course with other vegetables.

Variation: You can also fry some ground meat with the onion, spices, etc., before adding vegetables. The dish then becomes peppers stuffed with meat and vegetables. You can bake this version with a cup of tomato sauce poured over the top.

Mixed Vegetable Pilau

2 T. butter
1 onion, diced
1 tsp. ground cardamom
½ tsp. ground coriander
¼ tsp. ground cloves

1 cup rice
1 can or 10 oz. frozen mixed
   vegetables, thawed
2 cups water or chicken broth

Fry onion in butter until it becomes soft. Add spices, stir, and cook for a minute more.

Add rice and stir until it takes on a good color and begins to brown.

Add vegetables. Add water or broth, and stir to mix ingredients.

Bring to boil, reduce heat, cover, and simmer for 20 minutes.

Variation: Thin slices of meat or chicken can be added along with the rice. For this version, you can also add a handful of raisins and/or roasted cashews or peanuts. You now have a main course to go with some achar, bread (chapatti or flour tortilla), and salad to make a full meal.

Noodles with Vegetables

You can make the above dish using rice noodles instead of the rice.

Prepare as above, but soak thin rice noodles in hot water until they become pliable. Drain them, and add to cooked onion and spices in place of the rice. Fry for just a minute or two, then add vegetables and broth. You can also add some thinly sliced cooked meat or chicken with raisins or nuts at this point. Cook only until dish is hot through.

Tibetan Pulled Dumplings (Thenthuk)

These are sometimes used in place of rice as a basic starch dish.

Simply mix 2 cups of flour with about ⅔ cup of water and a little salt to make a firm dough. You can add ½ tsp. baking powder to make lighter dumplings. Knead the dough for a few minutes to activate the gluten. If the dough becomes sticky during kneading, sprinkle on a little more flour.

Separate the dough into 8 balls, rub a little oil on them, cover, and let rest for 15 to 30 minutes.

While dough is resting, heat 4 cups water or broth in a Dutch oven.

Roll dough into long strips, flattening to about 1 to 1½ inches wide.

Here is the "pulled" part: Hold a flattened strip in one hand, and with the fingers of the other pull off about an inch at a time, flattening the dumplings still more between your fingers as you pull. Drop pieces as you pull them into the pot of boiling water or broth.

Cook for 5 or 6 minutes until dumplings are done. Drain and serve with curries, etc.

Variation: As dumplings cook, you can add thin strips of meat, spinach, etc., to the broth (use broth, not water, for this). Season with salt and pepper and other spices as desired, and serve as a hearty soup.

Note: If you add chicken to the dumplings and broth you get something very similar to the Southern chicken and dumplings (page 73) in the North America section. In fact, I remarked to my wife that pulling rather than cutting the dumplings seemed to be the major difference. Her response: "But Mom always pulled her dumplings!" Again, we're not as far apart as we thought.

Spicy Spinach

This is essentially cooked spinach as we know it, but the onion and spices give it a characteristic Indian-Nepalese "kick."

2 T. butter	¼ tsp. ground cumin
1 onion, diced	¼ tsp. ground turmeric
½ tsp. grated fresh ginger	10 oz. frozen spinach, thawed

Fry onion in butter until softened but not browned. Add ginger and spices, stir, and cook for a minute or two more. Stir in spinach, add a little water, and simmer 12 to 15 minutes until spinach is cooked.

Note: You can, of course, use a pound or more of fresh spinach for this if you prefer.

Mushrooms

A Nepalese cookbook says to put turmeric on mushrooms and let stand for several minutes. If the turmeric turns black, the mushrooms are poisonous, so don't eat them. I suppose we don't have to worry about that with mushrooms from the local market, but it's an interesting claim anyway (just *don't* try it).

Fry a diced onion in butter with 1 tsp. minced garlic and ½ tsp. minced fresh ginger. Add some hot chili pepper if you like. Stir in 1 cup of sliced mushrooms, and continue frying until mushrooms are browned.

Orange Lentil Dal

"Dal" is the name for any dish of cooked legumes. You can use any color lentils, but the orange ones are pretty.

1 cup dry lentils	½ tsp. turmeric
2 cups water	1 tsp. ground cinnamon
½ tsp. salt	1 tsp. ground coriander
2 T. butter	¼ tsp. ground cloves
1 onion, diced	1 tsp. garam masala
	salt and pepper to taste

Soak lentils in water to cover for about an hour. Drain, and discard water.

Add ½ tsp. salt and enough fresh water to cover. Bring to boil, and cook until lentils are tender and most of the water is absorbed. (This may take a half hour or longer, but check after 15 minutes.) Add more water if needed.

Fry onion in butter until it is lightly browned. Stir in spices and cook for a minute or two more.

Stir onion and spice mixture into lentils. Check for seasonings, and serve as a side dish with main courses or over rice as a light meal.

Cabbage with Potatoes

2 T. butter
1 onion, diced
½ tsp. turmeric
1 tsp. ground coriander
½ tsp. fenugreek or cardamom

2 potatoes, sliced or diced
2 cups thin sliced cabbage
2 cups water
salt and pepper to taste
fresh mint (optional)

Fry onion in butter. Add spices, stir, and cook for a minute. Add potatoes and cabbage, stir, and cook for 2 or 3 minutes.

Add water and some salt and pepper. Reduce heat, cover, and simmer for about 20 minutes. Stir occasionally and add more water if needed. Check that potatoes are done. If not, cook a few minutes more. Check seasonings.

Serve with a garnish of thinly sliced fresh mint if you like.

Cauliflower Curry

Compare this with a similar dish from South Africa (page 177). Both are very tasty.

1 head fresh cauliflower or 2 (10 oz.) boxes, frozen	¼ tsp. ground cumin
	½ tsp. ground turmeric
1 potato, sliced	1 tsp. garam masala
2 T. butter or oil	1 tomato diced
1 onion, diced	2 cups water
2 tsp. garlic, chopped	salt and pepper
½ tsp. grated fresh ginger	

Clean and cut up cauliflower, or thaw frozen. Boil potatoes for about 10 minutes, drain, and set aside.

Fry onion in butter or oil until it begins to brown. Add garlic and ginger. Stir and cook a minute longer.

Add cumin, turmeric, and garam masala. Stir, and add cauliflower and potato. Stir and fry for 2 or 3 minutes. Add tomato.

Add water, reduce heat, cover, and simmer for 10 minutes or until vegetables are tender. Stir occasionally, and add more water if necessary. Check for seasonings, and serve.

Variations: You can use all cauliflower or all potato for this recipe also. Some recipes call for adding ½ cup plain yogurt just before serving, especially with all potato curry.

A similar dish calls for using tofu and peas. Prepare as above, but fry tofu along with onion, and add peas at the end. Cooking time will be less for peas.

Sweet Potato Fried Bread (Parotha)

Chapatti bread (like a flour tortilla) is common here as elsewhere in most of the world. This is a sweeter and intriguing alternative.

2 cups flour	1 cup mashed cooked sweet potato
½ tsp. salt	
1 tsp. baking powder	1 T. sugar
2 T. vegetable shortening	1 tsp. ground cardamom
1 cup water (approx.)	½ tsp. cinnamon
	salt to taste

Mix salt and baking powder with flour, and rub in shortening with your fingers until it is well distributed. Slowly add enough water to make a medium dough. Sprinkle on a little more flour if you get it too wet. Divide into 4 balls and set aside.

Mix sugar and seasonings into cooled sweet potato.

Make a hole in each dough ball, fill with potato mixture, and press edges to seal completely. Gently flatten to form a round, and fry in butter until browned on both sides.

Another way is to halve each dough ball and roll out flat. Place filling on one round, top with the other, and seal edges. Cook as above.

Orange or Lemon Squash
(Sherbat)

Do not be misled by the name. This is a soft drink and has nothing to do with summer or winter vegetables. "Squashes" are popular in many countries, and the name presumably comes from the fact that you must "squash" the fruit to get the juice out.

In Nepal, squashes are supposed to be good to prevent heat exhaustion in the hottest part of the summer.

Take 2 cups of fresh orange or 1 cup of lemon or lime juice, and boil with 2 cups water and 1 cup sugar. When sugar is dissolved, allow liquid to cool slightly and stir in 1 T. citric acid (available in health food stores). You can also add some food coloring if the shade of the drink isn't bright enough. Bright orange or yellow seems to be preferred to "natural."

Serve in a glass over ice. Add a sprig of fresh mint for garnish if you like.

Rice Doughnuts
(Sel)

Sweets are appreciated in North India and Nepal, but desserts are generally served with meals only on very festive occasions. Compare these with the version given in the Tanzania section (page 204).

1 ripe banana	½ cup powdered sugar
1 cup rice flour	1 T. melted butter
1 tsp. baking powder	

Mash banana to a paste and add to rice flour with baking powder, sugar, and melted butter. Add enough water a little at a time to make a thick batter (a little thicker than usual pancake batter).

Heat a pan with an inch or more vegetable oil in it to medium high heat. Drop batter by heaping tablespoons into hot oil.

Fry on both sides until light golden brown. Take them out when they are not quite as brown as you think they should be. They get a little darker as they cool.

Drain. Dust with powdered sugar and serve. (I don't know if this is strictly authentic, but a little cinnamon mixed with the sugar would certainly be good.)

Corn Pudding

Sweet corn (maize) is not native to this region, but as in many parts of the world, it has been adopted into the local cuisine. This is a particularly nice use of this versatile food.

1 (15 oz.) can creamed corn
1 T. butter
½ cup dried cherries, cranberries, etc.
¼ cup milk (optional)
½ tsp. ground cardamom
¼ cup shredded coconut
½ tsp. cinnamon (optional)

Combine all ingredients in saucepot, and heat slowly until butter is melted and fruit is softened. Add the milk if you prefer a more liquid consistency. Serve in individual bowls. If desired, coconut can be sprinkled on top of servings instead of mixed in. Garnish with a little more cinnamon if you like.

Index

Appetizers
    Cheese spread (liptovský sýr), 2
    Fish spread, 156
    Pickled herring, 23
    Salmon spread, 83
    Scotch eggs, 61

Beverages
    Caribbean punch, 104
    Lovefeast ginger beer, 103
    Orange or lemon squash (sherbat) (fruit drink), 226
    Tangy fruit cream, 123

Breads. *See also* **Desserts**
    Biscuits: Caribbean (roti), 100
    Buns: Czech (kolačky), 20-21; Labrador (Mrs. Winter's "day" buns), 84; Nicaraguan, 153
    Chapatti bread, 185
    Dumplings: Knedliky, 12-13; North American, 72-73; Plantain (foo foo), 91; South African, 180; Spätzle, 36; Tibetan (thenthuk), 220
    Flatbread: cassava (bammie), 127
    Johnny cake, 101
    Pancakes: Alaska sourdough, 82; Dutch, 39
    Sweet potato fried bread (parotha), 225
    Tortillas: Honduran (pupusas), 128-29; Miskitu, 139

Chicken. *See* **Meats**

Condiments & relishes. *See also* **Sauces & seasonings**
    Mango relish: Caribbean (sombal), 102; North India (achar), 211
    Pickled red cabbage, 25
    Tomato relish (tomato achar), 211

Desserts. *See also* **Breads**
    Apricot mousse, 17
    Baked berry dessert, 83
    Banana dessert, 205
    Cakes: Cake of three milks (pastel de tres leches), 152; carrot, 182; chocolate (Sacher torte) (Sachrův dort), 18-19; ginger (parkin) 63; Königsfeld sponge, 43; Nicaraguan "coco," 149; orange, 181; strawberry torte, 42
    Caramel spread (dulce de leche), 148
    Coconut squares (dulce de coco), 151
    Coconut tarts (guizadas), 150
    Corn pudding, 228
    Custard sauce for tarts, 65
    Dutch pancakes, 39
    Fruit bars, 183
    Pies: chocolate, 85; coconut, 105; fudge, 86; mango, 106
    Rice doughnuts: North India (sel), 227; Tanzania, 204
    Rice pudding, 123
    Sisters' kisses, 44

Strudel, 38
Sugar cake, 87
Trifle, 64-65
Zwetschgenkuchen (Bad Boll plum tart), 40-41

Dips & spreads. *See* **Appetizers**

Fish. *See* **Meats**

Fruit
Baked Nicaraguan ripe plantain, 145
Fried plantains with cream (plátanos fritos con crema), 145
Fried plantains, 90

Meats
Antelope (kudu), 174
Beef: and broccoli, 116; braised (Sauerbraten), 30; braised with sour cream (svíčková na smetaně), 6; country style steak, 76; and curry, 217; fried steak, 77; grilled steak (carne asada), 144; meat rolls in tomato sauce (Spanish birds) (Španělští ptaci), 9; roast and Yorkshire pudding, 48-49; veal paprika (telecí maso na paprice), 8
Chicken: in coconut milk, 190; in cumin sauce, 191; and curry, 172-73, 215; and dumplings, 72-73; fried (Tanzanian), 193; and groundnuts and tomato, 191; and paprika (kuře na paprice), 8; and pepper sauce (piri-piri), 192; pies, 68-69, 171; and potatoes (Bauernschmaus or farmer's treat), 29; and rice, 113, 136-37; roasted, 170; salad, 157; and spinach, 216; yam stuffed, 114-15
Chipped beef on toast, 81
Fish: baked, 164; blue trout (forelle blau), 28; braised, 189; and chips, 50-51; in coconut milk, 165; Creole rice with codfish, 112; curried (matjeri masala), 111; fish cakes, 51; fried, 214; pickled herring (Rollmops or Matjes), 23; pudding, 95; salt fish, 94; sole with parsley sauce, 57; stew (rondon (rundown)), 135
Goat, curried, 98
Meatballs: Frikkadelle, 162-63; with capers (Königsberger Klopse), 31
Meatloaf: Daddy's, 74-75; quiche (bobotie), 175
Pies: British, 52-53; chicken, 68-69, 171; Cornish pasties, 54; hot meat pies (empanadas), 130-31; Labrador meat pie, 80; meat triangles, 158-59; sambusas, 186; samosas (little pies), 212-13
Pork: baked chops, 166; roast pork (vepřová pečeně), 7
Sausages: British, 58; German, 32
Shepherd's pie, 55
Tamales (nacatamales), 132-33
Tanzanian roast meat, 195

Pancakes. *See* **Breads**

Salads
Chicken salad Port Elizabeth, 157
Chinese salad, 119
Cucumber salad (okurková salát), 3
Mixed Salad, 24
Moravian slaw, 69
Onion and tomato salad, 210
Pineapple salad, 156
Plain salad (hlávkový salát), 3

Index

Seafood. *See* **Meats**

Sauces & seasonings
Rubs and marinades, 96-97
Spicy peanut sauce, 108
Tanzanian curry powder, 188
Warm bacon dressing, 70

Snacks
Brootjes (little sandwiches), 32
Cabbage and cracklings snack (vigoron), 138
Fried cheese (smažený sýr), 10
Guava cheese, 102
Moravian Historical Society lunch, 71
Onion rings, Nepalese, 210
Pickled herring, 23
Ploughman's lunch, 60
Scotch eggs, 61

Soups & stews
Black bean soup (sopa negra), 126
Butternut squash soup, 160
Callaloo (tropical soup), 92
Chicken soups: and cheese, 161; Javanese (saoto), 109; or partridge, 78
Fish stew (rondon (rundown)), 135
Meat stews: caribou stew, 79; and cassava soup, 110; goulash (gulášová polévka), 4; Irish, 57; lamb and orange, 118; Lancashire hot pot, 56; pepper pot soup, 93; and potato (bredie), 176; potjiekos, 168-69; Tanzanian, 194-95
Pea soups: Dutch, 27; lentil, 179
Potato soup, 26
Tomato soups, 46-47, 209
Vegetable soups: North India, 208; white soup (bílá polévka), 5

Vegetables
Asparagus (Spargel), 37
Beans: and rice, 140-43, 196-97; on toast, 62
Bok choy, braised, 122
Broccoli, and beef, 116-17
Cabbage: braised, 200; braised (zelí dušené), 15; creamed, 70; pickled red cabbage, 25; and potatoes, 37, 223
Cassava (yucca): flatbread, 127; fried, 147
Cauliflower: and curry, 177, 224
Corn tamales (tamales de elote), 134
Cornmeal mush: fungi, 99; pap, 180; ugali, 187
Eggplant with curry (mchuzi wa biringani), 201
Greens and potatoes, 199
Lentils and peas: orange lentil dal, 222
Mixed vegetables: creamed (zeleny na smetaně), 16; and noodles, 219; pilau, 219; roasted, 178; samosas (little pies), 212-13; Tanzanian succotash, 200; stir fry, 202
Mushrooms, 221
Onion rings, Nepalese, 210
Pepper: stuffed bell peppers, 218
Potato salad 34; with cheese sauce (papas a la huancína), 146
Potatoes: boiled (Brambory), 11; and cabbage, 37; cheese-stuffed (brambory plněné sýrem), 11; and chicken (Bauernschmaus or farmer's treat), 29; curried (alu tarkari), 120; dumplings (Klösse), 35; fish and chips, 50-51; fried (pommes frites), 33; and greens, 199; pancakes

(Kartoffelpuffer), 33; roasted, 59
Pumpkin, stewed, 122
Rice: and beans, 140-43, 196-97; and chicken, 113, 136-37; Indonesian rice cakes (lontong), 121
Sauerkraut, sauteed (dušené kyselé zelí), 14

Spinach: and chicken, 216; groundnuts (peanuts), 198; spicy, 221
Sweet potato fried bread (parotha), 225
Yams and chicken, 114-15
Yucca (cassava): flatbread, 127; fried, 147

Around-the-World Moravian Unity Cookbook was written and composed on Microsoft Word computer program. Printed and bound by Edwards Brothers Corp., Lillington, North Carolina.